"As a former CFO, now an executive leader of a large nonprofit, I found that this makes for a great read to recalibrate my thinking and find greater balance between mission impact and financial return. We, as leaders of social change organizations, are driven by our heart and passion—this book allows for thoughtful and deliberate analysis to evaluate and develop a business model that propels our mission and strengthens our organization while never compromising our philosophies. Executive directors and their board leadership will find this book invaluable—a remarkable resource in assessing and planning their nonprofit's future success."

—**Gloria Aguilera Terry,** president, Texas Council on Family Violence

"At last! An urgently needed framework to prepare leaders to meet head-on the persistent twin challenges of impact and sustainability. This is a practical tool based on good business principles that can bring boards and staff members together to lead their organizations to sustainable futures."

—**Nora Silver,** adjunct professor and director, Center for Nonprofit and Public Leadership, Haas School of Business, University of California, Berkeley

"Up until a few years ago, funding and managing a nonprofit was a bit like undertaking an ocean voyage. You plotted your course, loaded provisions, and set sail. Now, it's akin to windsurfing—you must be nimble, prepared to maximize even the slightest breeze, and open to modifying your course at a moment's notice. Innovative executive directors or bold board members who want their organization to be able to ride the big waves of the new American economy must read this book."

—**Robert L. E. Egger,** president, DC Central Kitchen/Campus Kitchens Project/V3 Campaign

"This book should stay within easy reaching distance and end up completely dog-eared because it walks the reader through a practical but sometimes revelatory process of choosing the right mix of programs for mission impact and financial sustainability. I have used this matrix ever since CompassPoint first published on it and believe, especially considering changing conditions, that its use is a practice in which every nonprofit should engage its board once a year."

—**Ruth McCambridge,** editor in chief, *The Nonprofit Quarterly: Promoting Spirited Nonprofit Management*

Nonprofit Sustainability

Nonprofit Sustainability

MAKING STRATEGIC
DECISIONS FOR
FINANCIAL VIABILITY

Jeanne Bell

Jan Masaoka

Steve Zimmerman

JOSSEY-BASS
A Wiley Imprint
www.josseybass.com

Published by Jossey-Bass
A Wiley Imprint
989 Market Street, San Francisco, CA 94103-1741—www.josseybass.com

Readers should be aware that Internet Web sites offered as citations and/or sources for further information may have changed or disappeared between the time this was written and when it is read.

Jossey-Bass books and products are available through most bookstores. To contact Jossey-Bass directly call our Customer Care Department within the U.S. at 800-956-7739, outside the U.S. at 317-572-3986, or fax 317-572-4002.

Jossey-Bass also publishes its books in a variety of electronic formats. Some content that appears in print may not be available in electronic books.

Library of Congress Cataloging-in-Publication Data

Bell, Jeanne, date.
  Nonprofit sustainability: making strategic decisions for financial viability/Jeanne Bell, Jan Masaoka, Steve Zimmerman.
        p. cm.
  Includes bibliographical references and index.
  ISBN 978-0-470-59829-0 (pbk.)
  1. Nonprofit organizations—Finance.   2. Nonprofit organizations—Management.   I. Masaoka, Jan.   II. Zimmerman, Steve, date.   III. Title.
  HD62.6.B45 2010
  658.4'012—dc22

                                                                              2010026640

Printed in the United States of America

FIRST EDITION
PB Printing   10 9 8 7 6 5 4 3 2 1

CONTENTS

TABLES, FIGURES, AND EXHIBITS

TABLES

FIGURES

EXHIBITS

One of the most profound questions a nonprofit can ask itself is "Who is our constituency, and what does it need our organization to be?"

This book is dedicated with heartfelt gratitude and admiration to all the people in nonprofits who ask this question, and who know that financial sustainability must be accounted for in the answer.

CompassPoint
NONPROFIT SERVICES

Jeanne Bell is CEO of CompassPoint Nonprofit Services (www.compasspoint .org), one of the country's leading providers of training and consulting services to nonprofit organizations, based in the San Francisco Bay Area with a national practice. Jeanne is a nationally respected consultant, researcher, and speaker on nonprofit finance, strategy, and executive leadership matters. She is coauthor of *Financial Leadership for Nonprofit Executives,* and her other research includes *Daring to Lead: A National Study of Nonprofit Executive Leadership, San Francisco's Nonprofit Sector,* and *Securing the Safety Net: A Profile of Community Clinic and Health Center Leadership in California.* Jeanne is board chair of the national Alliance for Nonprofit Management and serves as a board member for the Nonprofits' Insurance Alliance of California and Intersection for the Arts. She has an M. A. degree in nonprofit administration from the University of San Francisco, is co-founder of the Finance Professionals Network, and is a frequent contributor to nonprofit journals.

www.blueavocado.org

Jan Masaoka is director and editor in chief of *Blue Avocado,* an online magazine for nonprofits that has sixty thousand subscribers (www.blueavocado.org). She served as executive director of CompassPoint Nonprofit Services for fourteen years, in which position she was named Nonprofit Executive of the Year by the *Nonprofit Times* in 2003. Jan is an eight-time designee as one of the national nonprofit sector's fifty most influential people, and in 2005 she was named California Community Leader of the Year by Leadership California. She is the author of *The Best of the Board Café* and *All Hands on Board: The Board of Directors in All-Volunteer Organizations.* Her research includes studies on nonprofit leadership, women executive directors of color, all-volunteer organizations, and the nonprofit workforce. She lives in San Francisco, speaks frequently on nonprofit-sector issues, and is a frequent contributor to nonprofit journals.

Steve Zimmerman is principal at Spectrum Nonprofit Services (www.spec trumnonprofit.com) in Milwaukee, where he provides consulting to community-based organizations in the areas of finance and strategy and works with staff and boards to better understand and strengthen their business models. Steve also speaks frequently and conducts trainings nationally on these subjects. Prior to starting Spectrum, Steve was a projects director with CompassPoint Nonprofit Services, where, in addition to training, he consulted on management issues to organizations whose revenues ranged from $250,000 to more than $20 million. He has also served as chief financial officer, development director, and associate director at other nonprofits. In addition to being a certified public accountant, Steve has a B.A. degree from Claremont McKenna College and an M.A. degree in business administration from Yale University.

Nonprofit Sustainability

**PART ONE**   # Introduction to Key Concepts

In Part One of the book, we explore the key concepts of sustainability, decision making, and strategies for nonprofit organizations. Chapter One offers an overview of what is covered in the book, describes how the topics are organized, and discusses how different audiences may use the book in different ways. Chapter Two introduces you to the three fictitious organizations that are used throughout the book to illustrate a variety of business model concepts.

Who Will Find This Book Useful, and How?

This book is about sustaining financial health and mission impact over time. Today, nonprofit leaders are deeply challenged by an array of complex, changing, urgent pressures that demand faster, smarter decisions than ever before. Success cannot be driven—or measured—by long-term, detailed plans and by whether those plans were carried out as written. Instead, community nonprofits sail in stormy seas where changing conditions mean a new route must be plotted every day. And on board these tossing ships is precious cargo: the lives of people in our communities, and the spirits and hearts of communities themselves.

For nonprofits, financial sustainability and programmatic sustainability cannot be separated. It's not enough to have a high-impact program if there's no effective strategy for sustaining the organization financially. And neither is it enough to be financially stable: we build our organizations for *impact*, not for financial stability.

Yet surprisingly, in the nonprofit sector financial information and information about mission impact are seldom discussed in an integrated way. Instead, financial reports and analysis rarely include data about what impacts have been driven by a particular financial activity. Moreover, program evaluations and progress reports are discussed out of context with funding streams, profitability, and financial sustainability.

This book's key premise is that financial and impact information can and must be brought together in an integrated, fused discussion of strategy. On that premise, in Part Two of this book we introduce a tested tool—the Matrix Map—as well as a perspective on and orientation to leadership and decision making. The following illustration shows how the Matrix Map leads to better decisions that in turn lead to a sustainable nonprofit organization.

Getting to Nonprofit Sustainability

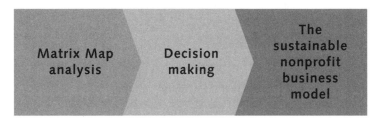

HOW THIS BOOK IS ORGANIZED

This book is designed around the understanding and regular adjustment of a nonprofit's business model, both of which are essential to sustained impact. We offer a number of practical concepts and tools for understanding the component parts of a business model and determining the optimal adjustments for improved mission and money results. These concepts and tools—put to use as part of a strategic planning process, in between strategic plans, or even in place of strategic planning—will help leaders make decisions that hold mission and money front and center in an integrated way.

The book is divided into five parts, described in the sections that follow.

Part One. Introduction to Key Concepts

Part One contains two chapters. In Chapter One, which you are now reading, we orient you to how the book is structured and discuss how different audiences will find the book useful. In Chapter Two, we define and discuss new ways to understand business models, sustainability, and financial viability in a nonprofit context. We also introduce the three fictitious nonprofit organizations that will serve as case studies throughout the book.

Part Two. Mapping Your Business Model: The Matrix Map

In the four chapters that make up Part Two, we identify and group programs and revenue lines, and then use the Matrix Map to analyze them for relative mission impact and for relative financial impact on the organization. The result is the expression of the organization's business model as a single, comprehensive, and compelling visual image.

Part Three. Making Choices to Adjust the Business Model

Once we have the mapped, de facto business model in view, the next steps, discussed in the three chapters contained in Part Three, are analyzing the individual parts *and* the whole and making strategic choices for program and fundraising activities. Part of doing so involves developing alternatives that may not have surfaced immediately.

Part Four. The Business Logic of Nonprofit Income Types

In the two chapters that comprise Part Four, we take a deeper look at the most common types of nonprofit income. This analysis is helpful to organizations considering new income strategies. It also illustrates the wide variations in how income is structured—and, as a result, it shows how different types of income need to be managed to different benchmarks.

Part Five. Ongoing Decision Making and Leadership

The two chapters in Part Five explore how success with a business model involves more than having a plan, and more than monitoring with that plan in mind. Success also requires attention to three areas for which we provide a perspective: an emphasis on execution, an orientation toward continuous decision making, and a differently understood role for leadership.

WHO WILL FIND THIS BOOK USEFUL, AND HOW?

Because of this book's focus on strategy and decision making, many nonprofit executive directors (CEOs) and other organizational leaders will find its concepts helpful in their demanding roles. Management teams will also find the book useful in both conceptual and practical ways as together they confront significant organizational decisions.

Nonprofit boards are also an important audience for this book. Too often board members know quite a bit about all the parts of the organization—its six programs and its two special events, let's say—but don't have a good way to understand the organization as whole. This book will enable them literally to see the organization's program and financial strategies in an easy-to-grasp visual image. And, after really grasping the comprehensive business strategy, they can act in more informed, strategic partnership with their executives.

Although we touch on process steps, this book is not organized around process guidelines, such as "Form a cross-department committee." Each organization evolves intentionally and unintentionally along its own path, and we leave it to each reader to develop an appropriate process for his or her organization.

We do, however, suggest different levels of intensity with which to engage these concepts. In some cases, a group can develop a quick Matrix Map (see Part Two) for a series of activities in less than an hour. In other cases, quantitative tools and analysis can be brought into play over a period of weeks or months. We'll suggest different ways to use these concepts, but our focus is on the concepts, ideas, and tools rather than on prescriptive process steps. Exhibit 1.1 offers notes to readers serving in a variety of nonprofit roles.

Let's get going.

Exhibit 1.1. Notes to Different Types of Readers

NOTE TO THE EXECUTIVE DIRECTOR/CEO

One area of tension for the person at the head of a nonprofit organization is a gap between a sense of where the organization needs to go and an inability to get the organization to move fast and intelligently. There are highly developed processes and frameworks for planning that are designed for consensus building, but an effective leader needs processes and frameworks for making faster decisions and for challenging the board and management team to look at bolder and more urgent questions than those often raised in a more leisurely planning process.

As an executive, you are likely to have many ideas for what the organization should be thinking about, but you may be uncertain about how to bring those discussions to the various circles within the organization. Part Five, on decision making and leadership, provides some ways for you to think about the role of the executive in leading decisions, ways that may be different from those you have read about before. In particular, Part Five focuses on understanding the processes by which business analyses, business plans, and strategic decisions are created and carried out.

NOTE TO MANAGEMENT TEAM MEMBERS OTHER THAN THE EXECUTIVE DIRECTOR/CEO

Management team members often like the phrase "Plan the work, then work the plan." In this light, they sometimes view their executive directors with both admiration and annoyance. On the one hand, the executive director has great ideas. On the other hand, she always seems to be starting new projects while disregarding what's already in the work plan. Or an executive director is great at "the vision thing," but he doesn't understand what it would take to implement a new program.

An underlying question for some management team members is often "How effective is the X program anyway?" As long as a program has enough funding, few management teams seriously question whether it should continue. But even when management team members do have opinions about the relative importance and impact of a program, they seldom have the venue or the circumstances in which such issues can be explored authentically.

Every organization makes decisions differently, and so every organization will use the Matrix Map differently (see Part Two). Nevertheless, we believe that management teams will find the Matrix Map especially useful as a way to raise deeper questions about strategy and impact, questions that often fail to get onto agendas that are already crowded with staffing issues, budget cuts, and program coordination. We also hope that you will find Part Five useful in your role as a program

(Continued)

director, an administrative director, or a leader serving in another management position. Decision making and leadership have an even greater presence *within* an organization's departments than at the top of the organization.

NOTE TO BOARD MEMBERS

One of the difficulties—and one of the pleasures—of serving on a nonprofit's board is being involved in a field that is new to you. Your day job may be in banking, but your board may oversee an organization devoted to autism. You may work in corporate human resources, but your organization is involved in wetlands restoration. Just as a clinical nurse practitioner may not know much about business models for advertising firms, board members may be newcomers to the business models of various conservation strategies.

Lack of experience with nonprofit income models can make it particularly difficult to participate fully in discussions about possible new ventures. If, for instance, a consultant or the executive director proposes a substantial investment in developing a mail donation campaign, it's hard for a person without knowledge of such campaigns to make an informed judgment about whether the investment is worthwhile.

This entire book will be useful to board members, but Chapter Ten, on nonprofit income models, may be especially helpful to board members and others who want to know the basic business logic behind such nonprofit vehicles as direct mail, major gifts, planned giving, and fees for service.

In addition, because this book bridges the gap between finance and mission, it will also help bridge the gap between nonprofit executives, who often intuitively and implicitly bring mission and money together in their minds, and boards, which function best when discussions explicitly bring concerns to the surface. One or two board members may find themselves constantly bringing up concerns related to the organization's financial sustainability, only to be seen by others as giving insufficient weight to mission-related goals. The frustration on both sides of this dynamic can be turned into positive energy through the use of the Matrix Map (see Part Two).

NOTE TO FUNDERS AND CONSULTANTS

Like nonprofit executives, funders and consultants also struggle with the need for plans that unify mission and goals on the one hand with financial realities and sustainability on the other. In particular, consultants with backgrounds in finance often tend to overemphasize conventional financial projections, whereas too many consultants in the area of strategic planning focus on consensus-building processes but lack the financial skills to bring financial perspectives productively into play.

You can use the Matrix Map (see Part Two) as a tool for strategic planning, and you can also use it to look more closely at sustainability in the context of a completed strategic plan. The Matrix Map incorporates financial information in a way that makes it easy to use even when board members, the executive, and consultants don't have backgrounds in finance.

A common role for funders and consultants is to give nonprofit grantees and clients guidance in developing plans for sustainability. It is our hope that the perspective presented in this book will be helpful to you in your own work, and in your role as a trusted advisor to nonprofits.

———— SUMMARY ————

Each chapter in this book concludes with a brief summary of the chapter's main points. In the case of this chapter, the main point is that nonprofit organizations, in order to be financially and programmatically sustainable, must combine their financial and programmatic dimensions in an integrated strategy. This book, written for leaders of nonprofit organizations, introduces an orientation to that integration as well as practical tools for its accomplishment.

Two Aspects of Sustainability

Every decision that nonprofit leaders make affects both the programmatic and the financial sustainability of an organization. Should we increase the size of our Head Start program? What should we do about our youth classes' loss of funding? Should we hold our dinner-dance this year? Where should I spend my time today? In some moments, boards and senior management may think of these decisions as being only about programs or finances, but every decision is about both. Finding the best allocation of time and resources to accomplish the organization's mission is a fundamental question and tension within each organization. When nonprofit leaders understand both aspects and hold them both in mind, they can make the best, most strategic decisions for an organization—decisions that will lead to ongoing programmatic and financial sustainability. Taken together, programmatic impact and financial viability are what make nonprofits sustainable.

CORE PRINCIPLES

This book takes the following as its core principles:

• *Financial sustainability.* Nonprofit emphasis on real-world impacts and on mission alignment is fundamental, but the separation of impact goals from financial goals and strategies has been a deep flaw in both business planning and strategic planning within the nonprofit sector. Financial sustainability is not only a legitimate goal; it is a necessary, intrinsic, core goal.

• *Hybrid revenue strategies.* Nearly all nonprofits now are hybrid organizations rather than traditionally funded charities: they combine donations, earned income, contracts, grants, and other income types. As a result, different financial goals must be set for different types of income streams, and they must be managed in significantly different ways.

• *Development of an explicit nonprofit business model.* Every nonprofit has a business model, whether or not it has articulated its strategy as such. Each program and fundraising line must be managed individually, but this must be done in the context of an overall integrated business strategy. Leadership's role is to develop and communicate that overall strategy as one that brings together all the activities—which will have different financial goals—into a viable business model. Unlike other approaches where contributed income (donations) and earned income run in separate areas within the organization, the business model described in this book intentionally integrates these two types of income in the context of overall financial goals. We also discuss the usefulness of business model statements, which, like mission statements, serve to summarize and remind organizational leaders of their core goals and strategies.

• *Continuous decision making.* Today's nonprofits face constantly changing situations that require decision making and choice making at all levels of strategy. The global economic crisis has underscored the reality that the environment changes in unexpected and unpredictable ways. Internal changes—the departure of a key staff person, for example, or a program's becoming stale—also demand decisions. In addition to detailed projections, leaders need a compass to support constant decision making.

WHAT IS SUSTAINABILITY?

Most of us in the nonprofit sector are familiar with setting programmatic goals. For instance, we might set a goal of reducing high school dropout rates by 10 percent in our community, or a goal of increasing the quality of the observations of one hundred amateur astronomy clubs. Nevertheless, we often aren't sure what our *financial* goals are, or even what they should be. If the financial goal in a for-profit company is to maximize profit, should our goal be to have no profit? Or should it be to grow an endowment of $10 million, or to have a profit of 5 percent?

In classical economics, the answer to this question is that the financial goal of a nonprofit is to ensure that it has adequate working capital; that is, its financial goal is to have enough money to do its work over the long term. Today we often use the term *sustainability* for this goal. But the term is used in different ways to suggest various things. Foundations and social entrepreneurs often describe a plan for sustainability as one that relies on earned income rather than on donations (although both earned income and donations can support long-term financial viability). When strategic plans are said to include goals for sustainability, what is often meant is that the plans include the goal of developing a more diversified income base. And environmentalists describe sustainability in terms of practices that are nonpolluting and that conserve energy and natural resources.

We like the United Nations' definition of *sustainability*: doing what is required "to meet the needs of the present without compromising the ability of future generations to meet their own needs" (http://www.un.org/documents/ga/res/42/ares42-187.htm). And we like the Wikipedia definition of *sustainability*: "the capacity to endure" (http://en.wikipedia.org/wiki/Sustainability).

In this book, we emphasize two critically important aspects of sustainability:

1. Sustainability encompasses both *financial sustainability* (the ability to generate resources to meet the needs of the present without compromising the future) and *programmatic sustainability* (the ability to develop, mature, and cycle out programs to be responsive to constituencies over time).

2. Sustainability is an *orientation*, not a destination. Sometimes the phrase "sustainable business model" sounds as if it refers to a place that, once reached, will allow the organization to generate financial resources on an ongoing basis while the board and staff sit back, relax, and watch it happen. But what is sustainable today may be unsustainable tomorrow. Funding streams dry up or shift focus; programmatic practices evolve; client populations change. We never arrive at a mix of programs and revenue streams that can be described as permanently sustainable. But we can always be heading in the right direction.

In practice, achieving sustained financial stability and mission impact means having leaders make major decisions while holding both objectives—as well as those two objectives' deep interconnectedness—front and center at all times. What do we mean by the term *interconnectedness*? Consider the example of a community center that cannot simply discontinue its annual neighborhood festival because of skyrocketing city permit and security costs. It has to consider the degree to which the community depends on the festival to promote local business and improve trust among neighbors. It also has to consider how its funders in city government would react to the festival's cancellation, given how much the funders use the festival as a venue for showing local responsiveness. There are simply *no* major decisions that do not have simultaneous implications for mission and money.

Good planning, be it strategic planning or business planning, is necessarily undertaken at intervals and is based on various assumptions and trends. In a rapidly changing environment, long-range plans may not provide sufficient guidance for managers and leaders. As the landscape changes, and as the nonprofit organization's capacity changes, the plan's assumptions as well as its objectives may become questionable or even irrelevant. The tools presented in this book are not intended to be used in embarking on yet another strategic or business planning process. Instead, they are meant to be used in the context of goals and plans that may become, to varying degrees, more or less possible than they were when the plan was formulated.

Despite the field's separation of tools for program analysis from tools for financial analysis, both aspects of nonprofit strategy are constantly on the minds of nonprofit leaders. As a result, financial considerations inform the thinking of executives as they guide planning processes, and impact considerations inform discussions about budget cuts. Yet there have not been tools that bring these two kinds of consideration and thinking together in a structured, systematic way, one that allows discussions to be more fully shared and explicitly critiqued.

The Matrix Map, introduced in Part Two of this book, is a tool that maps both the mission impact and the financial viability of an organization's activities, providing a visual image of the organization's business model in a manner that will foster discussion, provide strategic options for the board and staff to consider, and ensure that decision makers hold to both aspects of sustainability as they make decisions.

CASE STUDIES: THREE ARCHETYPAL NONPROFITS

To paraphrase an old saying, every successful nonprofit organization is successful in a unique way. Failed nonprofits may look similar to one another, but a nonprofit's success often depends on a unique set of circumstances and uniquely adept decision making. This is all the more true to the extent that a nonprofit organization reflects and serves the needs of its surrounding community (see Exhibit 2.1). As we move through various tools, it will help to have a few archetypal organizations to consider along the way. We'll use these archetypes to illustrate how the tools can be used in organizations of different sizes and with different activities, and to demonstrate that organizations can make decisions in strikingly different ways and still be successful.

Exhibit 2.1. Nonprofits and Community

We believe in nonprofit organizations as critically important, and critically integrated, components of healthy communities. Our society justifiably places a high value on our large nonprofit institutions, including universities, hospitals, research institutes, and housing developers.

Community nonprofits come in large as well as small sizes. Many community nonprofits are small but others have annual budgets of more than $30 million. Other community nonprofits with small budgets have large volunteer forces.

Perhaps more important, such organizations are not only the vehicles for how our communities take care of themselves, they are the engines for social change. For example, just think about the origins of the following important social movements and concepts:

- Civil rights for people of color

- The women's movement

- The environmental movement, including work on cleaner air and water

- Participatory decision making in organizations and companies

- Interactive and group student learning

- Rights for people with disabilities

- Valuing the arts at many levels beyond the classic institutions

- Patients' involvement in their own medical decisions and care

These and countless other movements and concepts were born, nurtured, and grew to maturity in the community nonprofit sector.

The three organizations we'll follow throughout this book are fictionalized composites to which we've given alliterative names so they will be easier to remember:

• *Midtown Multiservice Center*, a human services organization with a budget of $12 million. Midtown has a staff of seventy-five. Its key programs are a Head Start preschool, ESL classes, U.S. citizenship classes, and an annual street festival. Its fundraising activities are a street festival and an annual campaign.

• *Tempest Theater*, a Latino community theater with a budget of $600,000. Tempest has a permanent staff of five. Its key programs are drama workshops for teenagers and ten Latino-themed dramatic performances per year. The theater's fundraising activities are a gala dinner-dance and solicitation of contributions from major donors.

• *Everest Environmentalists*, an environmental conservation and advocacy organization with a budget of $2 million. Everest has a permanent staff of twenty-eight and a volunteer force of one hundred. Its key programs are environmental restoration, environmental education, a plant nursery, and site rentals (for birthday parties). Everest's fundraising activities are the site rentals along with a direct mail campaign, solicitation of contributions from major donors, and an annual event.

We'll also bring in other examples from our consulting work as we present the options and implications of this decision-making framework.

SUMMARY

Rather than a destination or a solution, sustainability is a direction and an orientation. Sustainability requires continuous decision making that reflects the dynamic context in which nonprofits operate. A nonprofit's strategy for sustainability must encompass both of the following two types of elements:

• Programmatic elements (meaning that the nonprofit's programs are relevant to its constituents and are having an impact)

• Financial elements (meaning that the organization has sufficient working capital for its needs and activities)

The Matrix Map is a tool for better understanding and pursuing sustainability.

 **PART TWO** # Mapping Your Business Model: The Matrix Map

Part Two introduces the Matrix Map, a tool for creating a comprehensive and compelling visual picture of an organization's current business model. Mapping the current business model is itself a powerful step in understanding the organization's strategies and how they fit together. As discussed in Chapter One, the Matrix Map will aid the organization's leaders as they constantly make big and small decisions that support sustainability.

To create a Matrix Map, we will first identify the business and programmatic components of the organization and then analyze each of these components in terms of its external impact on the community and its internal impact on the organization's finances.

Getting to Nonprofit Sustainability

We begin, in Chapter Three, by identifying the organization's core activities, or business lines. In Chapter Four we determine their profitability, and in Chapter Five we examine their relative impact. Finally, in Chapter Six, we use the Matrix Map to create a visual representation of the organization's current business model.

Identifying Core Activities: Business Lines

Business decisions are made not in the abstract but in the context of an existing business model, regardless of whether that business model has been articulated. We don't decide *hypothetically* whether a community center should have classes in English as a second language (ESL), but whether Midtown Multiservice Center should have ESL classes. ESL classes, and the resources they both require and generate, are part of Midtown's business model. Midtown's mission may sound similar to that of hundreds of other community centers around the country, but the unique mix of activities and revenue streams that has evolved at Midtown over the years is just that—unique. It is Midtown's business model.

In order for leaders at Midtown to make good decisions about the ESL classes, or about any other activity in Midtown's portfolio, they need to have a strong, comprehensive, and current grasp of the organization's full business model and of the relative implications of continuing to invest in ESL classes. The analysis of those implications is the key ingredient of a good business decision.

Let's use a well-known for-profit example to make this point about unique business models and their implications for good business decision making. Think for a moment about two very successful companies—Target and Williams-Sonoma. Both sell cookware. Target sells inexpensive cookware through large stores in outlying areas, and it advertises through newsprint inserts in local newspapers.

Williams-Sonoma sells expensive cookware through boutique stores in high-rent districts, and it advertises through glossy, full-color catalogs mailed to high-income zip codes. Each company has put together a winning formula based on the particulars of its business model. But what if Target were to try selling its colanders and measuring spoons at the same prices that Williams-Sonoma charges? (Would you buy a colander for $60 at Target?) Or what if Williams-Sonoma were to mail newsprint flyers instead of glossy catalogs to its high-end customer base? Neither decision would yield positive financial results.

Similarly, every community nonprofit has a business model. That is, every nonprofit has a set of core activities that it executes, and strategies for obtaining the necessary funds to do so. Many nonprofit leaders have an intuitive sense of these business strategies. That intuition is certainly invaluable to a successful organization. At the same time, leaders' intuition is often not well articulated, and so it is hard for others to participate effectively in shaping the organization's future. Articulating the current business strategies and how they fit together to shape the organization's business model is an important part of educating others in the organization and equipping them to partner with the executive director in strategic decision making.

The first step in making the business model explicit is identifying the organization's core activities, or business lines. We use these terms interchangeably and suggest that you pick the one that best engages your staff and board in this kind of business thinking. Core activities are represented by the groups of essentially similar products, services, and revenue-generating vehicles that make up the organization's overall effort. In a nonprofit, services are not always purchased or paid for by the consumer, and so some business lines may be programmatic only, whereas others may be focused on generating revenue. For instance, at Midtown Multiservice Center, there are two types of business lines—programs and fundraising activities. The programs include a preschool, the ESL classes, and an annual street festival. One of the organization's fundraising activities, which raises unrestricted funds, is an annual campaign for donations. Table 3.1 shows the business lines in each of the three fictitious, archetypal nonprofits featured in this book's case studies.

How we elect to group products, services, and revenue-generating activities necessarily affects how we come to see, analyze, and make decisions to strengthen the business model. When leaders first identify business lines, there may be some debate about where certain activities live. For instance, you will note that at

TABLE 3.1
Business Lines of Three Nonprofits

Midtown Multiservice Center	Everest Environmentalists	Tempest Theater
Core Activities		
Head Start preschool	Environmental education	English-language performances of plays originally in Spanish
ESL classes	Restoration/ reforestation	Performance of Spanish-language plays
U.S. citizenship classes	Plant nursery	After-school drama workshops
Annual street festival	Resource library	
Quit Smoking classes		
Revenue-Generating Vehicles		
Annual campaign	Site rentals	Newsletter
	Direct mail	Special events
	Solicitation of major donors	
	Annual event	

Tempest Theater the leaders separated the English-language and Spanish-language plays. Although one could argue that all the plays could be grouped into a core activity called "productions," leaders determined that the two sets of plays have very different audiences and impacts and therefore need to be understood as distinct business lines. This was not so much a question of what was right or wrong as of what the theater's leaders wanted to examine. Thanks to the conversations that led to this decision, the theater's staff and board now have a shared and more nuanced understanding of the theater's business model.

Another challenge in grouping core activities may involve location. Many nonprofits have similar programs spread across multiple sites. When that is the case, leaders have to decide whether the dominant business questions are around the sites or around the programs themselves, regardless of where they are offered.

Again, there is no right or wrong here, just the need for leaders to come to an agreement about what is most important to analyze. In this situation, they may decide that both kinds of analysis are needed in order for leaders to understand the organization's business model in terms of both site-specific and purely programmatic concerns. If a natural grouping does not immediately emerge, one approach is to try focusing on the external side of things rather than the internal side. For instance, look at how your marketing efforts describe your core work, or at how you group services when you approach a funder with a request to invest in them.

Volunteer Solicitation and Management

One of the common, important, and often overlooked aspects of a nonprofit's success is its use of volunteer labor. Volunteer labor is a large donated resource, which, like all donations, requires staff time to solicit, acknowledge, and manage well. Volunteers' time is also a resource that is "spent" in large amounts on program work, fundraising, and other activities. Like other large expenditures, its management takes staff time. If volunteers' time is a substantial resource whose solicitation and management requires significant staff time, should volunteer solicitation and management be regarded as a business line in its own right?

There is not a single clear-cut answer to this question. Rather, it's a case of navigating through the gray zone. For example, a youth organization's after-school program includes both tutoring and a sports league. Volunteers from the community do much of the tutoring, and the organization's staff members spend time recruiting, screening, and placing the volunteers with appropriate students. Of course, the time it takes to coordinate all of this costs money in the form of staff salaries, but it is far cheaper than having to hire paid tutors, and it arguably brings a different—and better—kind of individual to the work. When this youth organization decides on its business lines, its leaders are looking at after-school tutoring, a sports league, individual donors, and a fundraising event. The cost of running the volunteer program is part of the after-school tutoring business line, since the volunteer program is not the business line itself but the delivery method for the tutoring.

The strategic question that is being asked, together with the decision that has to be made, may help in determining whether volunteer solicitation and management should be pulled out as a separate business line. This youth organization is considering starting an advocacy department to promote more money for education and after-school programming. The organization has good data as well as stories of the impact that the organization has had on its constituents' lives, and the leaders feel that, with the voices of the volunteers who are helping in the tutoring program, they will be able to change public policy effectively. In this scenario, it would make sense to pull volunteer management out as its own separate business line because the volunteers are serving two purposes: not only are they delivering a core program for the organization by tutoring, they also represent a broad base of support to bolster the organization's advocacy efforts. Closing the volunteer program would affect not just one but now two business lines of the organization, and so volunteer solicitation and management should be seen and maintained as a separate business line.

Like other business decisions, the decision to split out volunteer solicitation and management is subjective. The organization should do what the staff and the board may feel most comfortable with, using whatever data will help them make a strategic decision for the organization's sustainability.

IDENTIFYING IMPACT AND REVENUE STRATEGIES

We said earlier that sustainability is a concept involving both financial health and programmatic impact, and that leaders are constantly attending to both. Therefore, a community nonprofit's business model *is* different from that of a for-profit business because programmatic impact strategies are an explicit part of it. An impact strategy is a plan for the external effects to be sought through a particular business line. A revenue strategy is the means by which a particular business line is financed. Each core activity in the business model is associated with both an impact strategy and a revenue strategy. This is why we say that every nonprofit has a dual bottom line—impact and financial return.

TABLE 3.2

Impact and Revenue Strategies at Tempest Theater

Business Line	Impact Strategy	Revenue Strategy
English-language performances of plays originally in Spanish	Entertain and challenge English-speaking and bilingual audiences, using Latino cultural, economic, and other relevant themes	Season and single-show ticket sales
Performance of Spanish-language plays	Entertain and challenge Spanish-speaking and bilingual audiences, using Latino cultural, economic, and other relevant themes	Season and single-show ticket sales
After-school drama workshops	Engage young people in the theater; provide positive options for at-risk kids; build an audience	Parent fees and city contracts
Newsletter	Market plays and workshops; elevate the profile of local actors and playwrights	Individual donations and season ticket sales
Special events	Build a community of donors and supporters; raise unrestricted funds	Ticket sales and auction

Table 3.2 shows how we would identify the impact and revenue strategies for some of the business lines at Tempest Theater.

The individual products and services, the grouped core activities, and the impact and revenue strategies together constitute the community nonprofit business model. Put simply, the business model is what we do, why, and with what resources.

THE PREMISE OF THE DUAL BOTTOM LINE

With the business model—inclusive of impact and revenue strategies—articulated, leaders can shift to analysis and then to decision making. The premise of the analysis

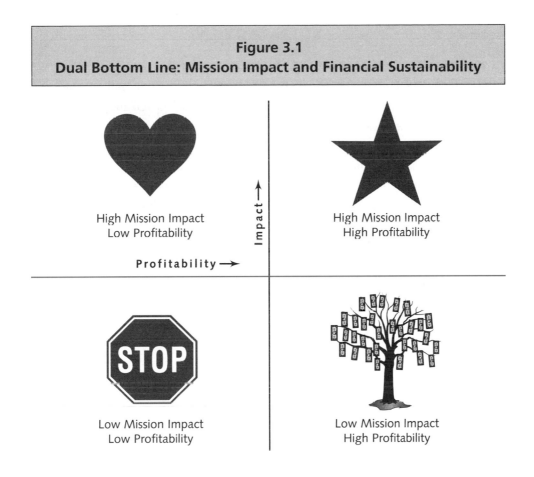

Figure 3.1
Dual Bottom Line: Mission Impact and Financial Sustainability

High Mission Impact
Low Profitability

High Mission Impact
High Profitability

Impact →

Profitability →

Low Mission Impact
Low Profitability

Low Mission Impact
High Profitability

that we will outline in the coming chapters is the dual bottom line in terms of which nonprofits manage—mission impact and financial return. We suggest that all activities need to be assessed on both their mission impact and their financial sustainability, as shown in Figure 3.1. At any given moment, a community non-profit may have an activity portfolio with activities spread across the four quadrants shown in the figure. Locating activities in these quadrants—what we call creating a Matrix Map—will suggest a clear set of decisions that leaders need to make in order to foster the business model's overall strength. (The icons that appear in the four quadrants of Figure 3.1—the Heart, the Star, the Stop Sign, and the Money Tree—are explained in Chapter Seven.)

SUMMARY

"Making the unconscious conscious" is a phrase that psychologists sometimes use to describe their work. The process of identifying your organization's core activities (or its business lines), as well as the specific impact and revenue strategies of each one, is the process of bringing your organization's current business model to its conscious mind. To do this, leaders need to examine the organization's mix of products, services, and revenue-generating vehicles and then group them into core activities. In our work, just this process of grouping and naming can result in a deeper understanding of the business dynamics at work in a nonprofit. This understanding in turn can lead to improved reporting, communication, fundraising, and more. It also is the basis for the kind of dual-bottom-line analysis and decision making that leaders must undertake continuously.

Determining Profitability

E ach of the core activities in a business model has financial and mission-related results. As we investigate the roles that different activities play in the business model, we will need to assess performance on both bottom lines. Let's start with the financial bottom line—profitability.

WHY DO NONPROFITS HAVE TO BE PROFITABLE?

As we argued earlier, the financial goal of a nonprofit is sustainability—in financial terms, the maintenance of adequate working capital. *Working capital* is a term for the funds that a nonprofit can use to continue its operations. Working capital is used to manage daily operations, to get through cash flow disruptions, to allow for mistakes, and to invest in new opportunities.

Unrestricted cash reserves, or unfettered working capital, are particularly precious in nonprofits, which must operate nimbly and creatively within extraordinary funding constraints. For instance, organizations that rely on government funding often face severe cash shortages when invoices for reimbursements are paid many weeks or even months after due dates. State and county governments often impose unrealistic limits on overhead, requiring nonprofits to supplement the government funding with their own funds in order to stay afloat. Foundation funds, meanwhile, are often episodic restricted grants that frequently pay only the direct costs of a program, not its associated basic costs, such as rent and administration.

Nonprofits acquire and maintain working capital chiefly by saving, that is, by having years in which they bring in more than they spend. In other words, in order for nonprofits to acquire, maintain, and expand working capital, they must be profitable.

If We Need to Make Profits, Why Are We Called Nonprofits?

It's unfortunate that the nonprofit sector has been dubbed with such a misleading name. The term *nonprofit* probably comes from *not for profit*, a more explanatory (but old-fashioned) term. Another word for *profit* is *surplus*, that is, a surplus of revenue over expenses, and some nonprofits use this term as a way of avoiding the word *profit*.

Nonprofits are, of course, not prohibited from having surpluses or profits. But they *are* restricted in terms of what they can do with those profits. Whereas a for-profit corporation can distribute profits to its owners and shareholders, a nonprofit corporation must reinvest all its profits in the organization and its mission.

If surpluses—profits—are essential to building up even modest savings, then it stands to reason that every nonprofit has to have in its portfolio some activities that generate profit. Such activities might include a consumer-paid program, where the market will tolerate pricing that leaves a surplus. Or they might include a well-managed annual event that leverages donated space and services to generate profit on table ticket sales. In any case, *something* has to generate profits, both to subsidize programs that cannot break even and to build cash reserves and working capital. As a result, assessing the financial return—the profitability—of each core business line is essential to analysis and decision making.

There is a natural resistance in nonprofits to describing a program as losing money, or being unprofitable. Some people assume that unprofitable programs will be eliminated, but it's important to quash this superficial view of profitability at the beginning of any discussion related to the financial impact of a program. In fact, the very essence of the nonprofit business model is that some activities will be profitable and that others will lose money. As we go forward, we'll see how to take both impact and profitability into account in program selection.

We'll begin by determining the profitability of the activities of Everest Environmentalists. To start with, let's take a look at Exhibit 4.1, an organizational

Exhibit 4.1. Income Statement for Everest Environmentalists, Year Ending December 31, 2009

Contributions	$ 390,000
Fundraising events	135,000
Cost of fundraising events	(72,000)
Foundation grants	$ 326,000
Total contributed support	779,000
Government contracts	1,100,000
Rentals	15,000
Total earned revenue	1,115,000
Total income	**1,894,000**
Environmental education	810,000
Restoration and reforestation	530,000
Plant nursery	200,000
Resource library	14,000
Administration	176,000
Fundraising	230,000
Total expenses	**1,960,000**
Change in net assets*	**(66,000)**

*"Change in net assets" refers to the surplus or deficit of revenue with respect to expenses (that is, the profit or shortfall for the period).

income statement of the type that is probably familiar to most managers and board members. A quick glance at this organizationwide statement reveals that Everest did not operate at a profit in this fiscal year. In losing $66,000 it is depleting its cash reserves, leaving itself with reduced savings and working capital.

Organizational leaders will want to know which of a nonprofit's activities made money, which lost money, and which broke even. To determine the profitability of any given business line, we need to know two things: the full costs of the business line, and the income associated with the business line. First we'll look at the costs.

DETERMINING THE FULL COSTS OF A BUSINESS LINE

There are many methods that nonprofits use to calculate the full costs of a given program, fundraising activity, special event, or other activity. In the nonprofit sector, unfortunately, accounting for the costs of a particular organizational activity has been made more difficult by the lack of agreed-upon terminology and by unwise guidelines from some government agencies, some funders, and some companies that rate nonprofits. Nevertheless, the debate over the wisdom of these guidelines is a topic best left to another book. Here, in this section of the chapter, we provide an overview of how to cost an activity.

In order to understand whether a program or fundraising activity is profitable, it's important to include all the costs that legitimately comprise that program or activity. Full costs include both direct costs and a fair portion of shared costs.

Everest Environentalists, for example, when costing its environmental education program, must include the program's direct costs, but it must also include a share of the organization's rent, computer-related expenses, supplies, management costs, and other costs. If these costs are not included in the full costs, Everest will end up underestimating the costs of the program. The results of this underestimate may include lost opportunities for reimbursement, incorrect pricing of this activity, or the impression that the program is profitable when in fact it may be a financial drain on the organization.

To determine the full costs for the business lines we have identified, we need to make sure that every business line includes the following expenses:

- *Direct costs.* These are the costs directly attributable to the program. For a tree planting program, direct costs would include the trees, the cost of the staff members working in the program, and the cost of the trucks, buckets, and shovels used in planting the trees.

- *A fair share of common or shared costs.* These expenses are for costs incurred by multiple programs, such as rent, supplies, utilities, and staff time used for more than one program (as when staff members attend a conference and then apply their new knowledge to two programs).

- *A fair share of administrative costs.* These are the costs incurred by the accounting department, by the board of directors, and by staff who devote 100 percent of their time to overseeing the organization as a whole.

Table 4.1 shows how these costs are allocated for Everest Environmentalists. The table illustrates the allocation of common costs as well as administrative expenses, and we've demonstrated this allocation in order to emphasize an important point: that the full costs of the organization's programs will include both sets of expenses, even though most readers of nonprofit financial statements are used to seeing the common costs already allocated, as they are in the income statement shown in Exhibit 4.1.

Note, however, that even though incorporating a portion of administrative expenses is important in this kind of analysis, such costs often remain separate in budgets as well as on the organization's Form 990. More information on this allocation can be found in Exhibit 4.2, which offers special in-depth technical guidance to finance staff.

DETERMINING REVENUE

To determine whether a business line is contributing financial resources to the organization or being subsidized, we must assign revenues to business lines, just as we did with expenses.

In many cases, it is clear that funding restricted to a particular program or activity is revenue that supports that activity, or that earned income or fund-raising income belongs to a particular business line. For example, consider the following types of funding and revenue:

- Foundation funds restricted to Program A
- Earned income generated by Program A
- Proceeds from a walkathon fundraiser

TABLE 4.1
Determination of Full Costs, Everest Environmentalists

	Environmental Education	Restoration/ Reforestation	Nursery	Resource Library	Site Rentals/ Birthday Parties	Direct Mail	Solicitation of Major Donors	Annual Event	Common Costs	Administration
Direct expenses	746,300	488,300	184,300	12,900	8,300	147,400	59,000	66,300	160,000	162,200
Allocation of common costs	63,700	41,700	15,700	1,100	700	12,600	5,000	5,700	(160,000)	13,800
Total before administration	810,000	530,000	200,000	14,000	9,000	160,000	64,000	72,000	—	176,000
Allocation of administration	80,000	50,000	20,000	1,000	1,000	15,000	6,000	3,000	—	(176,000)
Full costs	890,000	580,000	220,000	15,000	10,000	175,000	70,000	75,000	—	—

Exhibit 4.2. Considerations for the Finance Staff

Allocating shared or common costs is a regular part of the finance and accounting staff's routine. Shared and common costs are those expenses shared between and among the different business lines. These are expenses such as occupancy, technology, insurance, office supplies, and other miscellaneous costs. They represent resources that are used by multiple business lines, and so the full costs of a business line must include its share of these expenses.

The most common method of allocating shared costs to a business line is to use the percentage of staff members (also called *full-time equivalents*) who work in that particular area. For instance, if a business line utilizes 26 percent of all staff time, then 26 percent of common costs would be attributed to it. Other common methods of allocating shared costs are to use as bases for allocation the square footage that each business line uses and the percentage of total payroll expense that each business line uses.

Most accounting software systems, such as QuickBooks and others, allocate shared costs right up front, basing them on percentages input at the beginning of the fiscal year. The same percentages can be used for our analysis, but you may need to split them out a bit more to make sure that all business lines are covered. For example, shared costs are simply allocated to "fundraising" and may not be broken down by business line. For our purposes, the total shared costs allocated to fundraising would need to be split into the various business lines, on the basis of estimates for each line.

To better capture the full cost of operating a business line, in addition to the direct and shared costs we also allocate a portion of the administrative costs of the organization. These costs are not allocated for presentation on the financial statement, but in grant proposals and government contracts they may be often included as overhead or indirect costs. The most common allocation method for administrative

(Continued)

costs is to use the percentage of total expenses that each business line incurs, which can be calculated with the following formula:

$$\frac{\text{business line's direct expenses} + \text{allocated shared expenses}}{\text{organization's total expenses} - \text{administrative expenses}}$$

Many foundations and government agencies place artificial caps on overhead. As a result, we're used to simply allocating 12 percent, for example, of overhead to a business line that has been funded with this guideline. Sometimes organizations do this without calculating their business lines' true percentages or costs. For our purposes, we are calculating the full cost, not what the government will reimburse. By allocating the administrative costs in the manner just described, we can see what the total cost of the business line is, as well as whether it is being subsidized or contributing income, and we can determine the appropriate strategic imperative to make our decision.

One last note on allocating administrative costs: Because these costs are not allocated for presentation on financial statements, most accountants find it easier to perform this step outside the accounting system, using a spreadsheet program such as Microsoft Excel. It may be easiest to keep allocations outside the accounting software to simplify interim statements.

In other instances, however, there may be less clarity about where to assign revenue. In fact, assignment of revenue is often confused by two issues.

First, it may be unclear whether a foundation grant should be assigned to the development department (which wrote the proposal) or to the program to which the funds are restricted. In this instance, the grant should be assigned to the program for which the funds will be used because these grant funds are revenue that supports that particular business line. In the case of unrestricted funds, they should be assigned to the activity or business line that was responsible for generating the funding. For instance, fundraising income from a walkathon is unrestricted, but if we want to understand the profitability of the walkathon (or any other fundraising activity), we need to assign the revenue to the event that generated it. Unrestricted revenue that is not tied to any particular activity (an event, a mailing, and so on) should be assigned to an "unrestricted funds" business line.

Second, it can be tempting to assign unrestricted revenue to programs that are losing money, in an effort to make those programs look as if they are breaking even. Try to resist this temptation—it's important to know the reality of a program's financial impact.

In some cases, it is necessary to make a judgment call about where to allocate revenue. Remember that although we want to be accurate, these numbers will not be audited, nor will the results be used to evaluate the performance of a particular employee (such as the development director).

In particular, judgment is required when there is "indirect revenue." There are two common situations in which this issue becomes complicated.

In the first situation, there may be a perception or an assumption that some unrestricted donations are made because of a particular program. At a community center, for instance, a major donor may be very fond of the annual neighborhood parade, and so any discussion of canceling the parade will be stopped short by someone saying, "But Mrs. X and her friends love the parade. If we cancel it, they'll stop giving." It's indisputable that some donors give because of one program or another, regardless of whether they legally restrict their gifts to that program or programs. What's difficult is to know whether those gifts will continue if the parade is discontinued, just as it's difficult to know whether a corporation will be willing to make its annual gift to a scholarship program rather than to a fundraising dinner.

In the second common situation in which it's difficult to assign indirect revenue, the revenue is from memberships that include bundled benefits. At one Asian historical society, for instance, a membership of $50 includes discounts to various events, an annual calendar, and an invitation to an annual members-only reception. It's not possible to "unbundle" the reasons why people join. Different members will value different parts of the membership package, and some may join without desiring any of the membership benefits at all. Stakeholder research may give us some clues to why people purchase memberships, but ultimately any answer to this question is a judgment call that will have to be made, and that will involve a decision about whether to stop including the calendar, for example, or about whether to add other benefits. It's also true that, over time, a particular membership benefit may begin to overshadow the original reasons for the organization (as, for example, when a civil rights organization offers health insurance to its members and it becomes clear, with 80 percent of the members completely inactive, that these inactive members joined solely in order to obtain health insurance). For the most part, community nonprofits offer memberships that are either mission-based (in which case the costs of member benefits should be seen as a cost of fundraising) or discount-based (in which case the lost revenue—discounted by, say, 20 percent—can be considered the cost of the membership).

In these types of situations, there is no single right answer for everyone. Just as one person could argue that revenues belong to one activity, someone else could argue with equal validity that they belong to another activity. These situations require leaders to make the best choices they can with the available information.

With such issues resolved in the case of Everest Environmentalists, Table 4.2 shows Everest's assignment of revenue by business line. And with full costs and revenue properly assigned to each business line, Everest's leaders can readily determine the current profitability of each of its core activities (see Table 4.3).

SUMMARY

To make good decisions about our activities, we need to understand how our activities' profitability (or need for subsidy) affects the overall financial health of the organization. Determining a business line's profitability requires us to calculate its full costs—direct activity costs, an allocated portion of common costs, and a further allocated portion of administrative costs associated with the activity. We also assign to each business line all the revenue directly attributable to it while allocating other resources to the fundraising activities that generated them. In Chapter Five, we'll turn to determining the mission impact of the organization's various business lines.

TABLE 4.2
Assignment of Revenue by Business Lines, Everest Environmentalists

	Environmental Education	Restoration/ Reforestation	Nursery	Resource Library	Site Rentals: Birthday Parties	Direct Mail	Solicitation of Major Donors	Annual Event	Administration
Contributions						220,000	170,000	135,000	
Restricted foundation grants	14,000	195,000	120,000						
Government contracts	900,000	200,000							
Fees					15,000				
Total revenue	914,000	395,000	120,000		15,000	220,000	170,000	135,000	

TABLE 4.3
Determination of Profitability, Everest Environmentalists

	Environmental Education	Restoration/ Reforestation	Nursery	Resource Library	Site Rentals/ Birthday Parties	Direct Mail	Solicitation of Major Donors	Annual Event	Administration
Total revenue	914,000	395,000	120,000	15,000	15,000	220,000	170,000	135,000	
Full costs	890,000	580,000	220,000	15,000	10,000	175,000	70,000	75,000	
Profit	24,000	(185,000)	(100,000)	(15,000)	5,000	45,000	100,000	60,000	

Determining Relative Impact

ith profitability determined, we now turn to the other bottom line: impact. Discussions about mission impact are often difficult to hold in nonprofit organizations. There's an implicit assumption that everything is important and that everything drives toward the mission. And that's usually true. But everyone also realizes—although people seldom say—that some programs have higher impact than others. We may avoid discussing different levels of impact in order to avoid sounding as if we are criticizing a worthwhile program (or its director). But it's precisely these judgments—about which are the highest-impact programs—that are used by impact-oriented senior managers as they choose, often subconsciously, where to spend their time. The dual-bottom-line analysis will bring these judgments into the light and allow leaders to make explicit decisions about where to deploy precious resources.

CHOOSING CRITERIA FOR IMPACT

One trap of analysis is to spend too much time working on criteria and on weighting these criteria in order to determine impact. The other trap of analysis is to spend too little time on devising and weighting criteria. In this section of the chapter, we'll provide seven criteria for consideration, but we encourage leaders to choose no more than four when evaluating relative impact. That way, leaders will avoid complicating the process to the point where the process—rather than the results—becomes the focus.

A word on objectivity: instead of trying to *eliminate* individual judgment in impact assessments, this method *harnesses* individual judgment that has been *informed by data*. For instance, the executive director's assessment of her organization's prenatal workshops for expectant mothers will be based on several factors, including the results of a longitudinal study of the program, her direct observation of the program, her knowledge of similar programs elsewhere, what she's heard clients say about the program, and so forth. It would be a mistake to ask her to use only the results of the longitudinal study to assess the program's impact. Instead, we want to make use of everything she knows, and to make use of everything that other members of the management team know.

FAST AGREEMENT ABOUT IMPACT

Sometimes people are already pretty much in agreement about which programs have the most impact. In such cases, a fast approach can work. The management team can simply discuss each program and business line briefly and then give each one a rating of 1 to 4:

1. not much impact

2. some impact

3. very strong impact

4. exceptional impact

For example, at an Underground Railroad home preserved by an all-volunteer organization, the group found it easy to identify the organization's business lines:

House preservation

Acquisition and maintenance of period furniture and decor

Living-history presentations

This group also found it easy to agree on the relative impact of each business line:

House preservation: 4 (exceptional impact)

Acquisition and maintenance of period furniture and decor: 2 (some impact)

Living-history presentations: 3 (very strong impact)

If the organization had unlimited resources to invest in its business lines, it might not have been important for this group to identify the relative impact of each one; the organization could have chosen to devote considerable attention to all of them. But when resources are limited, the right decision may be to take the resources going toward maintaining period furniture and redirect them toward preserving the house—the business line where the deepest impact is possible.

SEVEN CRITERIA FOR DETERMINING IMPACT

A more robust way of considering relative impact is to look more closely at the components of impact. The following seven criteria have been developed and tested in nonprofits. For each one, we offer illustrative examples as well as types of data that can be used in assessing the activity along each criterion.

Look again at the 1–4 ratings:

1. not much impact

2. some impact

3. very strong impact

4. exceptional impact

If we were to use only one criterion for impact—say, alignment with core mission—a rating of 4 would mean exceptional alignment with core mission, whereas a rating of 1 would mean not much alignment with core mission. Organizations can develop and choose their own criteria, but the seven that follow are those that have been the most successful for test organizations.

1. Alignment with Core Mission

Most (or probably all) current program activities are generally congruent with a nonprofit's mission, but they may not all be contributing to an increase in the specific impact(s) the organization currently pursues.

For instance, the Midtown Multiservice Center holds Quit Smoking classes for neighborhood residents and was recently recognized by state monitors for its exceptionally effective program. Although this program clearly has an impact on its participants, there is room for discussion about whether smoking cessation is relatively more aligned with Midtown's core mission than are the citizenship classes and the neighborhood parade.

The following information sources contribute to efforts directed at assessing the degree of a program's alignment with the organization's core mission:

- Program logic models or theories of change that articulate desired impacts and how programs lead to them
- Industry journals, standards, conference sessions, and other discussions of high-impact strategies

At Tempest Theater, the after-school drama workshops for teenagers were given a score of 3 on a scale of 1–4 for alignment with core mission. The theater primarily exists to bring audiences compelling dramas with Latino themes. Although the staff members come to enjoy and love the students in each class, they see the classes as subsidiary to the organization's key mission. The drama workshops help get families involved with the theater, and some of the students audition for the few youth parts in the plays. This is a very good program, but its alignment with the theater's core mission is not its strong point.

2. Excellence in Execution

Is this program or business line something that the organization offers in an outstanding, superior way? Do we execute this program competently, or do we execute it amazingly well?

Earlier we said that nonprofits often pay more explicit attention to planning than to execution. The criterion of excellence is a way of getting at execution. For instance, some conferences are much better than others, but all of them may have the same basic plans behind them. It is in the actual doing of the conference work—its execution—that excellence emerges (or doesn't). Excellence may also be closely tied to particular individuals, who may not be easily replaced if they leave. Assessment of excellence takes those individuals' unusual strengths (or flaws) into account.

The following are sources of information related to the criterion of excellence:

- Program evaluation data
- Feedback from customers, patrons, and clients
- Direct observation

- Staff performance evaluations (Do this program's staff members consistently deserve high marks?)
- Staff turnover and exit interviews (Do staff members believe that this program is excellent?)

To take another example from Tempest Theater, the after-school drama workshops also scored a 3 for excellence in execution. The classes are creatively and energetically taught, and the students respond. At the same time, the workshops are plagued with logistical problems—late preparation for classes, frequently unrealized plans to bring in guest performers, and so forth. In addition, the theater's artistic director teaches the classes, and because of her many responsibilities, she doesn't always have time to give this program her best efforts.

3. Scale or Volume

Does the program reach a large number of people? The same program will have a higher impact if it reaches two hundred people than if it reaches fifteen.

The following sources may provide information related to the criterion of scale or volume:

- Client utilization records (enrollment, page views, ticket sales, and so on)
- Products or services completed (birds rescued, books sold, legal cases won)

The drama classes at Tempest Theater are capped at fifteen students per class, and there are two classes per year. On the criterion of scale, the drama classes were given a 2.

4. Depth

Does the program have a high impact on the people involved? A program may not have scale, but it may have a deep impact on the thirty students it enrolls each year. In contrast, a program may touch a lot of people, but in a relatively light way. An environmental organization may see its deepest impact in the yearlong greening processes it completes with five manufacturing companies per year, whereas every day thousands of people see its provocative billboards promoting the benefits of a green economy. Nonprofits may purposefully keep a mix of scale and depth in their portfolios.

The after-school drama workshops at Tempest Theater were given a 4 for depth. The students who participate seldom have participated in cultural enrichment programs before, and most of them go home to empty houses or hang out somewhere when they are not in the classes. When they take the classes, they very often find themselves deeply moved and inspired about expression and about possibilities.

The following sources may provide information related to the criterion of depth:

- Program logic models or theories of change that articulate specific desired impacts and how programs generate them

- Program evaluation data

5. Filling an Important Gap (FIG)

Competition and alternative providers have important but subtle and indirect influences on impact levels. For instance, if there are many ESL classes in an area, an organization may give its own ESL program a relatively low ranking on the FIG criterion. The program's constituents may not like the other classes as much, but at least ESL classes are plentiful and available. However, if there are no other ESL classes in the area, and if a good many people desire them, then the same program may score a 4 on this criterion.

An organization may be the sole provider in an area, but that doesn't necessarily mean that the program being assessed should get a high score on the FIG criterion. It may fill a gap, but that gap may not be one that is really important. For example, Everest Environmentalists may be the only organization offering workshops on native plants, but these workshops may be assessed as filling a relatively unimportant gap.

The following activities may provide information related to the criterion of filling an important gap:

- Reviewing competitors' and alternative providers' Web sites and information

- Asking clients and constituents where else they obtain or could obtain the service in question

- Polling referral agents in the area (such as United Way, the school district, or others) to see where else they refer callers asking about this service or product

- Reviewing page 2 of competitors' and alternative providers' Form 990s (showing key program accomplishments and related expenditures)

At Tempest Theater, the drama workshops received a 2 on the FIG criterion. As much as staff members felt that the workshops were excellent, they didn't see them as crucial to the community. "It would be sad if they were discontinued," said one staff person, "but not disastrous."

6. Community Building

Does the program help build the community around the organization—the community in which the organization works? For instance, a botanical garden elected to maintain a weekday gardening lecture series, despite diminishing attendance, because the remaining attendees were longtime volunteers at the garden, and the classes were a meeting ground for them. To take another example, an organization's 2K Fun Run may not greatly increase fitness or raise much money, but it may be a popular event that brings families back to old Chinatown. In other words, one measure of impact may be related to building the capacity and strength of the community—its individuals, organizations, and field—rather than to building the organization itself. When an organization makes a contribution to building the communities and movements to which it belongs, this contribution is appropriately recognized as impact.

At Tempest Theater, the drama classes received a 3 for community building. The existence of the classes was well known in the Latino community, and the classes made a statement about the theater's commitment to youth. Many parents who attended student performances were attending a theater for the first time, and the staff got to know more families in the community.

The following sources may provide information related to the criterion of community building:

- Interviews with community and field leaders
- Reviews of donor histories
- Client/market surveys

7. Leverage

Programs, of course, do not exist in isolation. They operate in the contexts of their organizations and of their fields. As a result, one element of impact is *leverage*, the degree to which a program or business line increases the impact of other programs. In some cases, leverage comes about because, in the context of rising demand for similar programs, a particular program strengthens the organization's standing and ability to raise funds for other programs. In other cases, a program may score high on the criterion of leverage because it creates tools or audiences that then enable other programs to be effective.

Possibilities for leverage may appear in three general sets of circumstances:

1. When the demand and the funding for programs and services are growing rapidly in a field or a geographical area

2. When the products or the audiences developed in a program become important tools and audiences in other programs

3. When a program has marquee value, which is to say that the program gives the organization high and positive visibility and branding

We often make assumptions about a program's leverage without really knowing if our assumptions are on target. For example, a nonprofit organization dedicated to media training offered excellent workshops on getting stories in the press and on the Internet. The organization assumed that the workshop participants would think highly enough of the workshops to contract later on with the organization for communications consulting. But a fast look at the organization's last ten consulting clients showed that none of them had taken one of the organization's workshops. In short, the media workshops did not have much leverage after all.

In contrast, an organization for counseling homeless youth gave free (and hip) clothing to clients ("If your feet are cold, you can't think about much else"). When the organization questioned its clients, it was discovered that the clients used the free clothing to justify coming for counseling when they couldn't really admit to themselves that they wanted counseling. In other words, the clothing program had leverage value to the organization's core mission.

Tempest Theater, after going through the exercise of giving its after-school drama workshops an initial scoring, characterized the workshops as follows:

Alignment with core mission: 3

Excellence in execution: 3

Scale or volume: 1

Depth: 4

Filling an important gap: 2

Community and constituency building: 3

Leverage: 2

The board and staff then discussed the plays in terms of the same impact criteria. Ratings for the two programs are shown in Table 5.1.

As explained earlier, these seven criteria are examples of what organizations can use in assessing relative impact (although, for practical reasons, we suggest using no more than four). These criteria are a more structured reflection of the kinds of thinking that managers use in discussions all the time. For instance, one person may say that a program reaches two thousand people, and another may comment that it hardly affects those two thousand people at all. When the concept of impact is broken into its various components, a group discussion can be more productive.

TABLE 5.1 Impact Ratings, Tempest Theater		
	Drama Workshops	Plays
Impact Criteria		
Alignment with core mission	3	4
Excellence in execution	3	4
Scale or volume	1	3
Depth	4	2
Filling an important gap	2	4
Community building	3	3
Leverage	2	1
Average (Unweighted)	2.6	3.0

We encourage organizations to develop impact criteria that are meaningful to them. Here are some other examples of impact criteria that can be used:

- The degree to which a program or business line gets at root causes
- The degree to which a program or business line builds the overall movement and cause in which the organization is a participant

- The degree to which a program or business line promotes and preserves the organization's strong relationship with a strategic partner

- The degree to which a program or business line contributes to academic-quality knowledge creation in the field of the organization's activities

WEIGHTING AND SCORING

It isn't necessary to give different weights to the criteria, but doing so may provide further nuance and depth to the assessment process. For instance, Midtown Multiservice Center's management team might decide that depth is more important than breadth, whereas Everest Environmentalists may decide that breadth and scale are more important to building the overall environmental movement. If the scoring is being done through a surveying process, questions are developed to elicit scores in each of the four areas, and a weighted average is developed for each activity. Exhibit 5.1 shows a blank scoring sheet used by the management team of Everest Environmentalists, and the results of organizational leaders' impact assessment are shown in Exhibit 5.2. Table 5.2 shows the results for Everest Environmentalists with respect to profitability determinations as well as impact determinations.

The Politics of Weighting

In choosing the criteria, and in weighting the criteria (if weighting is done), it's possible for a group of people to stumble into some quicksand. Sometimes this occurs because people in nonprofits share a good trait—they care deeply about values, and weighting reflects values. For instance, some board members at Midtown Multiservice Center felt strongly that bringing the neighborhood together was one of the center's most important functions, and that the annual street festival did this more powerfully than the ESL classes. Other board members thought it was more important to have a deep impact on individual lives.

The sticky part of weighting is that people tend to use the weighting discussion to debate the value of programs instead of having discussions about the programs themselves. At Midtown Multiservice Center, for example, board members who argued that the criterion of community building should be more heavily weighted than the criterion of depth were seen by supporters of the ESL classes as making that argument just because community building was aligned with the street festival.

Exhibit 5.1. Impact Scoring Sheet, Everest Environmentalists

	1. Alignment with core mission: How closely does this activity align with our core mission?	2. Excellence: To what degree does this activity reflect the best work we do?	3. Filling an important gap (FIG): To what extent is this activity important? Is it the only one of its kind available to the community?	4. Community building: To what degree does this activity build the movement in which our organization works?
Environmental education				
Restoration and reforestation				
Nursery				
Resource library				
Direct mail				
Solicitation of major donors				
Annual event				
Site rentals				

Exhibit 5.2. Impact Assessment with Compiled Scoring, Everest Environmentalists

On a scale of 1 to 4, with 4 being the highest, please rate each business line on the four criteria listed below. As you complete your assessments, remember that there are no "right" answers, and take into account all the information you have from your experience with the organization.

	1. Alignment with core mission: How closely does this activity align with our core mission?	2. Excellence: To what degree does this activity reflect the best work we do?	3. Filling an important gap (FIG): To what extent is this activity important? Is it the only one of its kind available to the community?	4. Community building: To what degree does this activity build the movement in which our organization works?	Weighted Average
Weighting	35%	35%	20%	10%	
Environmental education	4	4	3	2	3.60
Restoration and reforestation	4	3	1	4	3.05
Nursery	3	1	1	2	1.80
Resource library	2	1	1	2	1.45
Direct mail	2	2	1	3	1.90
Solicitation of major donors	2	3	1	3	2.25
Annual event	1	2	1	2	1.45
Site rentals	2	2	1	1	1.70

TABLE 5.2
Profitability and Impact Scoring, Everest Environmentalists

Business Line	Profit or Loss	Mission Impact	Expenses
Environmental education	24,000	3.60	890,000
Restoration and reforestation	(185,000)	3.05	580,000
Nursery	(100,000)	1.80	220,000
Resource library	(15,000)	1.45	15,000
Site rentals	5,000	1.70	10,000
Direct mail	45,000	1.90	175,000
Solicitation of major donors	100,000	2.25	70,000
Annual event	60,000	1.45	75,000
Total	(66,000)		2,035,000

Acknowledge explicitly that weighting choices reflect values, and that the weighting discussion is an effort to find some balance that will not end up making every criterion of equal weight. The weighting discussion is a good place to start getting to the values discussion, but if weighting the criteria means that the values discussion gets bogged down, then it may be better not to give different weights to various criteria.

Guidelines for Scorers

Leaders may choose criteria, and they may choose to weight the criteria, but the process of assessment is one area of building your organization's Matrix Map that can involve as many or as few people as you wish. Online survey companies like Survey Monkey and Zoomerang make it relatively cheap and easy to draft a survey and send it to board members, members of the organization's advisory council, major donors, and other relatively large groups.

It is important for the individuals who participate in rating to understand their role. In particular, the survey instructions should focus on the following points:

• Tell survey respondents that you will use the compiled results as a *starting point*—not as the final word—for the decisions to be made about programs. Explain to your staff how decisions will be made (for example, by way of a proposal from the management team to the board of directors).

• Formal program evaluations that have already been conducted should be used to *inform* individual judgments, not substitute for them. This means that if an outside evaluator has conducted an assessment of a program, then each person responding to the survey should use the information from the evaluation but should also use his or her judgment about the accuracy or the approach of that evaluation.

• Ask respondents to bring everything they know to the assessment process. Some individuals may feel uncomfortable making assessments because they feel that they do not have in-depth knowledge of any particular program. Others may have experienced a particular program as that program's constituents, not as staff people, and still others may have been constituents as well as program staff members. Whatever the situation, encourage survey respondents to bring their whole selves to the process and to share their authentic feelings about the activity as opposed to what they think someone may want to hear, or what they themselves may have felt while they were in particular roles.

• Tell respondents, "Don't game the process." It may be tempting to give your own program a score of 4 on everything so it will have more points for averaging. But try not to give in to this temptation. Remember that scoring is an opportunity to think in a newly clear way about the different dimensions of a program's impact.

• Remind respondents that the assessment is about determining the *relative* performance of the organization's programs. This process is not about deciding which programs are good and which are bad. Rather, it is about acknowledging and collectively thinking through which programs have *relatively* more impact than others.

Who Should Participate in Scoring, and How?

Figuring out who should participate in scoring is a little like throwing a party. In some sense, there is a feeling of "the more, the merrier," but without your close friends, a party still feels somewhat empty. Similarly, when it comes to scoring your organization's impact, the more people who participate in the scoring, the merrier, but a high number of people does not necessarily make for a more accurate score.

Here are some of the groups who should be considered as participants:

• *The management team.* An expanded meeting of the management team may also take place for this purpose. When it's time to determine relative impact ratings, the organization's management team is a logical place to start. Management team members are used to working with each other and discussing programs. At the same time, however, people on management teams are typically chosen because they oversee various areas. As a result, sometimes the most strategic and thoughtful individuals in the organization are not on the management team. For instance, at a nonprofit radio station, two individuals who are important organizational thinkers and leaders—the news director and the chief engineer— may not be on the management team but can be invited to any management team meetings where the Matrix Map is being developed.

• *The board of directors.* Most board members are more familiar with some business lines than with others. The board also represents the community perspective and can be just far enough from the organization's details to provide an important perspective. Holding a discussion about scoring can be a highly effective way to engage board members in digging more deeply into discussions about programs, to awaken them to underlying questions, and to challenge them to think about each program and business line in a strategic way.

• *Other staff groups.* Staff members have a good understanding of the details and the impact of their business lines, and they typically aren't shy about sharing their opinions. It may be useful to have the staff members in each department assess their own programs but not other programs or business lines. For example, the development staff might do the first assessment of the various fundraising activities.

SUMMARY

To make a credible assessment of your current core activities' relative impact, the elements of impact that are relevant to your business model have to be selected as criteria. These criteria may include such factors as a program's depth, its breadth, its ability to fill a critical gap in your community, and its ability to leverage other programs or the field. When effectiveness and impact are unbundled, discussion and reflection are better able to inform judgments.

Engaging staff and board members in candid reflections on how the business lines are delivering on the organization's mission requires leadership— clear communication about how staff and board members can best participate, and a sense of safety as they offer their frank judgments.

Mapping the Matrix

Now that we've determined the relative profitability and the relative impacts of each of our core activities, we can build a visual model of our organization's current business model.

The Matrix Map is built on two axes: impact and profitability. Let's look first at how to map profitability (see Figure 6.1). Activities are placed on the Matrix Map so that those toward the left are less profitable than those on the right end of the line. In Figure 6.2, Program Y is a break-even program. Program X is less profitable and requires subsidy from the organization's unrestricted funds. Activity Z is more profitable and creates a surplus that can be used to subsidize other programs, or it can be saved in a cash reserve.

Business lines are moved up and down the vertical axis, in contrast, based on their impact (see Figure 6.3). In Figure 6.4, all three programs—J, K, and L—are break-even programs. However, J has relatively greater impact than K, and both have relatively higher impact than L.

In establishing the Matrix Map, we now have the ability to place each activity—whether a program or a fundraising activity—into one of the four quadrants shown in Figure 6.5.

Once we have determined impact and profitability for each activity, it is time to put them together on the Matrix Map. To map the matrix, create a grid with profitability on the x-axis (horizontal) and impact on the y-axis (vertical; see Figure 6.6).

With this information, we can create a Matrix Map for Tempest Theater (see Figure 6.7).

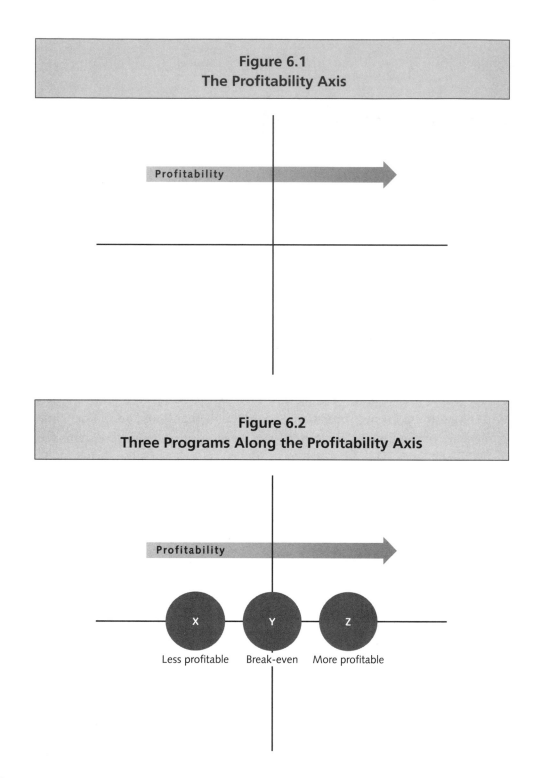

Figure 6.1
The Profitability Axis

Profitability

Figure 6.2
Three Programs Along the Profitability Axis

Profitability

X

Y

Z

Less profitable   Break-even   More profitable

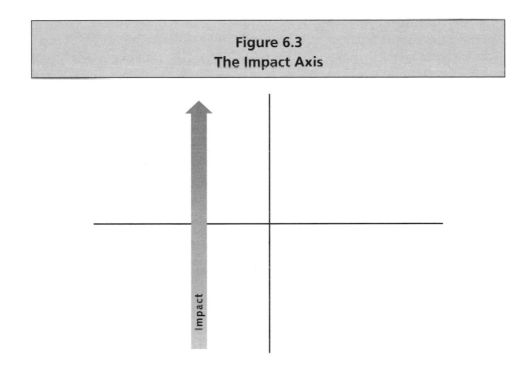

Figure 6.3
The Impact Axis

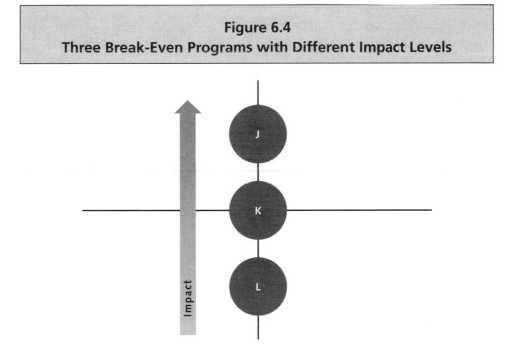

Figure 6.4
Three Break-Even Programs with Different Impact Levels

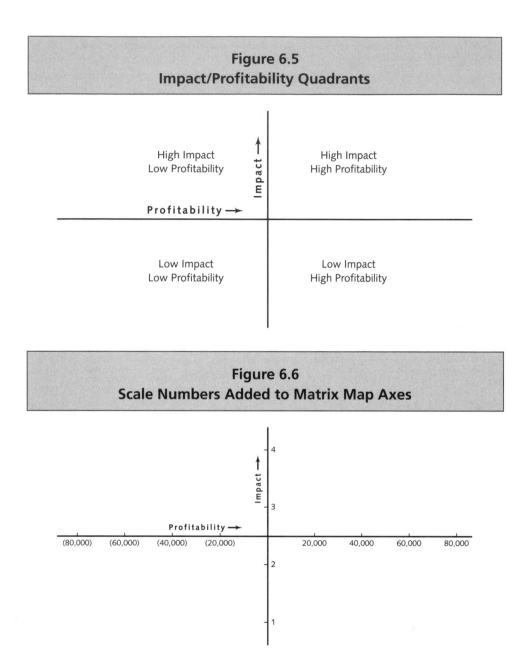

Figure 6.5
Impact/Profitability Quadrants

High Impact
Low Profitability

Impact →

High Impact
High Profitability

Profitability →

Low Impact
Low Profitability

Low Impact
High Profitability

Figure 6.6
Scale Numbers Added to Matrix Map Axes

Impact →

4

3

2

1

Profitability →

(80,000) (60,000) (40,000) (20,000)   20,000   40,000   60,000   80,000

Next we add shading. Programs are shown as dark gray, and unrestricted fundraising activities as a lighter gray. Tempest Theater now has an exceptionally clear and complete picture of its activities as well as of their relative impact and

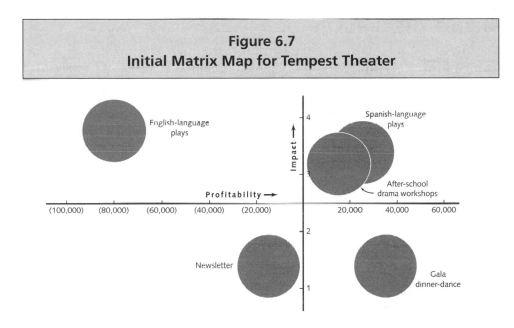

Figure 6.7
Initial Matrix Map for Tempest Theater

their relative financial impact/profitability, as shown in Figure 6.8. In Figure 6.8, however, each of the circles is the same size, unlike what we will see as we continue to build the Matrix Map.

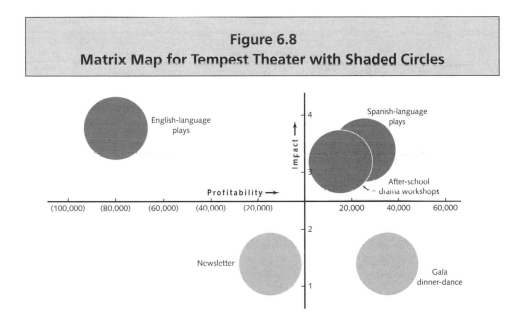

Figure 6.8
Matrix Map for Tempest Theater with Shaded Circles

SIZING THE CIRCLES

The last and critical step in building the Matrix Map is to make each circle or bubble for each activity on the grid correspond to the size of its expenses. When this step is completed, the Matrix Map not only allows you to see how each activity is contributing to your programmatic and financial sustainability but also allows managers and the board to see the degree to which resources are coming from and going to various business lines.

Once we change the sizes of the activity circles to correspond to their respective expenses, we've completed the Matrix Map, and the picture of the organization's business model emerges. Figure 6.9 is the completed Matrix Map for Tempest Theater.

Even before we get the strategic implications for each activity, we can begin to get a sense of how each activity contributes to the financial sustainability and mission impact of the organization, and we can start to see what may need to be done strategically. This method of mapping your core activities according to their impact and financial profitability, and then sizing the activities according to their expenses, can be used for any organization, regardless of its mission, its age, or the size of its budget. Conscious or not, these dynamics are in place at every nonprofit organization.

Figure 6.9
Completed Matrix Map for Tempest Theater

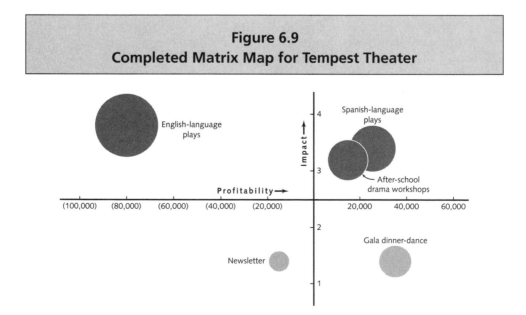

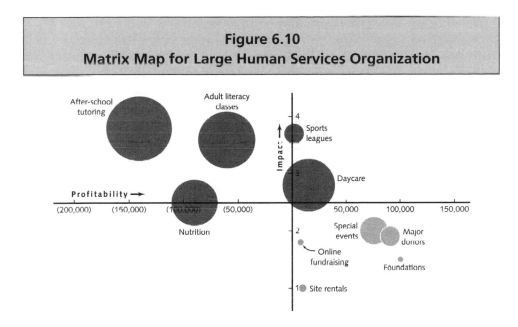

Figure 6.10
Matrix Map for Large Human Services Organization

In a moment, we'll show the completed Matrix Maps for our two other archetypal organizations, but Figure 6.10 is what a Matrix Map might look like for an even larger community organization. The organization represented in Figure 6.10 has ten core activities of varying sizes. Naturally, the larger an organization, and the more activities it has, the more crowded the Matrix Map will look. The more crowded Matrix Map does not signify, however, that the larger organization has more impact than a relatively smaller organization, just that it has more moving parts. Regardless of the number of activities or the complexity of the organization, the initial reactions to seeing your organization's business model can be very similar.

AHA! SEEING THE CURRENT BUSINESS MODEL

The power of seeing all the organization's significant activities in one unified graphic image is hard to overstate. Board members may be used to looking at financial information at every board meeting, but the Matrix Map dramatically shows how the core activities work together for financial and programmatic sustainability.

Here are some typical *Aha!* moments that board and staff may experience upon seeing the Matrix Map:

"Activity X is bigger (or smaller) than I thought."

"It's overwhelming (or impressive) how much we're doing."

"I never knew that X had a higher impact than our other programs."

"Now I understand why we spend so much time talking about fundraising. It is extremely important."

"Wow. *That* program is *really* fueling the organization."

At Tempest Theater, the board's review of the organization's completed Matrix Map (see Figure 6.9) was a revelation to board members in terms of the financial importance of the after-school drama workshops. The organization had never spent much time talking about the program and viewed it only as a tangent of the organization's core mission.

FROM *AHA!* TO THE BUSINESS MODEL STATEMENT

A business model statement is a useful companion to an organization's mission statement, in several ways. Just as a mission statement serves to remind everyone in an organization of the organization's core work, the business model statement helps remind everyone what the economic drivers are in the organization. Such reminders keep discussions and decisions on track.

A business model statement is not simply a list of funding sources, just as a mission statement is not simply a list of all the goals of the organization. An effective business model statement describes the strategy for financial sustainability, focusing on the key strategy and how it is linked to impact. In this chapter, we'll be looking first at business model statements for our three archetypal organizations, and then we'll offer a sampling of business model statements for a variety of other types of organizations.

The first draft of Tempest Theater's business model statement came out as follows:

> We produce plays and conduct youth workshops, sustained through a mixture of ticket sales, foundation grants, workshop fees, and an annual benefit.

This descriptive statement contains all the elements of the business model, but it doesn't call out either the program drivers or the financial drivers of the organization. It's adequate, but it could be stronger.

A more focused business model statement was developed:

> We produce Spanish- and English-language plays, supported by ticket sales and foundation grants, and supplemented by net income from youth workshops and an annual gala.

This is a clear, straightforward explanation of how Tempest Theater is financially sustainable. It states bluntly that youth workshops and the gala are supplemental to the production of the plays, which are the central purpose of the organization. As a result, the statement does not compromise the organization's mission or goals.

This business model statement is a touchstone, in the same way that a mission statement serves as a touchstone. Together, the mission statement and the business model statement speak directly to the organization's mission and its plan for programmatic and financial sustainability:

> *Tempest Theater mission statement:* Our mission is to celebrate, examine, and contribute to the Latino experience in the United States through high-quality theater for Latino and mainstream audiences.
>
> *Tempest Theater business model statement:* We produce Spanish- and English-language plays, supported by ticket sales and foundation grants, and supplemented by net income from youth workshops and an annual gala.

At Midtown Multiservice Center, the board was not surprised to see that the organization's current set of activities was not financially sustainable. However, board members were surprised to see the relative impact of each of the programs (see Figure 6.11). The board had always talked about the programs separately, never really thinking of them in relation to one another. Separately, the Quit Smoking classes seemed like a great program, but the board had never thought of them as having less impact than Midtown's ESL classes.

Midtown created the following business model statement:

> Midtown Multiservice Center serves our neighborhood through a Head Start program supported by a government contract, and

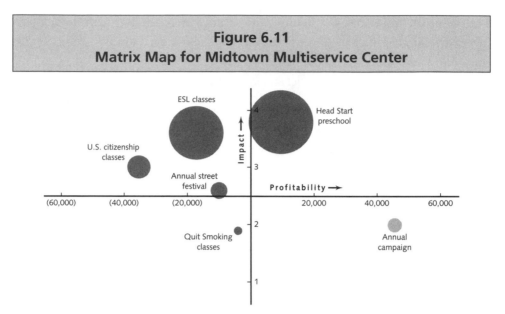

Figure 6.11
Matrix Map for Midtown Multiservice Center

through ESL classes, citizenship classes, and Quit Smoking classes supported through fees and an annual street festival with business sponsorships. This is all subsidized by the generosity of individuals through our annual campaign.

An immediate reaction to this draft was that it didn't include all the many activities of Midtown Multiservice Center, thereby making them seem unimportant. At the same time, although some of the smaller activities (such as renting rooms to Girl Scout troops) were important aspects of the organization, they didn't represent core programs or core business drivers. It was agreed to change "This is all subsidized" to "These and smaller activities are subsidized":

Midtown Multiservice Center's mission statement: Through service and partnerships, we serve and represent the people working and living in Midtown, and we strengthen our neighborhood's prosperity, diversity, and quality of life.

Midtown Multiservice Center's business model statement: Midtown Multiservice Center serves our neighborhood through a Head Start program supported by a government contract, and through ESL classes, citizenship classes, and Quit Smoking classes supported through fees and an annual street festival with business sponsorships.

These and smaller activities are subsidized by the generosity of individuals through our annual campaign.

While mission statements are typically published broadly, business model statements are more internal statements that will be shared with donors and other investors. Midtown is known as a large nonprofit, and the business model statement explains the organization's funding sources. It also explains the ways in which the mission statement translates into programs and activities, at least at this moment in the organization's history.

Exhibit 6.1 shows sample business model statements for a variety of nonprofit organizations.

Exhibit 6.1. Sample Business Model Statements

Health clinic: We are a fee-for-service health clinic supported by government contracts and supplemented by individuals and a variety of other small revenue streams, including patient fees and corporate in-kind donations.

Although the basic premise of the health clinic is that it uses a fee-for-service model whereby patients are charged for services received, the business model statement highlights that the government is the primary payer and that the services are subsidized by individuals.

Education reform organization: We are involved in research and advocacy for educational reform, supported by a few committed individual and foundation donors who helped create and share our vision for reform.

This education reform organization may receive lots of small donations, but it is primarily funded by a few individuals and foundations. Its business model statement helps to guide strategy and reinforces the importance of understanding the needs and interests of these individuals and foundations.

Association or coalition of providers: Our focus is on return value to members. We are led by members, supported by dues

(Continued)

---

from members, and supplemented by foundation grants for special initiatives.

This business model statement for a typical member-based association clarifies the strategic mandate to understand the needs of members and continue to provide value. It also recognizes the importance of external funding for special initiatives.

Soccer league: We are an all-volunteer youth athletics organization supported financially by dues from parents and sales of candy bars.

Many organizations survive on volunteer labor and have only a few expenses. It is important that business model statements capture both the importance of volunteers to the business model and the way in which the organization generates financial resources.

Local disease chapter: We raise awareness and research funds, supported by dedicated individuals who typically have been touched by the disease. We are also supported by corporations through a walkathon and direct mail appeals.

Again, nonprofit business models encompass both mission impact and financial viability. The business model statement for this organization illustrates how a local disease foundation accomplishes its mission programmatically, through research and awareness, and financially, through individuals and corporations.

Food bank: We distribute in-kind donations of food from corporations through volunteers, supported financially by major donors and community foundations.

In-kind contributions, similar to volunteer labor, play an important role for some nonprofits. This business model statement highlights the importance of in-kind corporate donations as well as volunteer labor.

Affordable housing development organization: We build affordable housing where government and developer fees are available.

The business model statement for this affordable housing development organization clearly articulates the conditions necessary for action.

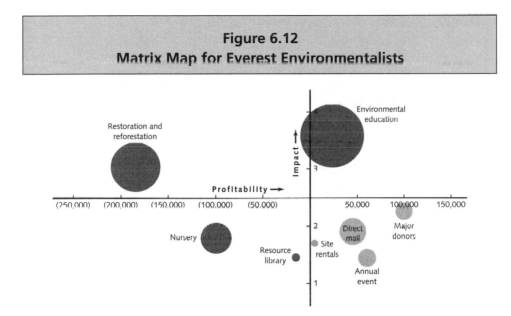

Figure 6.12
Matrix Map for Everest Environmentalists

The board and staff of Everest Environmentalists were a little overwhelmed with the number of activities that showed up on their Matrix Map (Figure 6.12). "No wonder we are so exhausted all the time!" exclaimed one board member. There were two other primary revelations that the board and staff of Everest experienced after seeing the Matrix Map. The first revelation had to do with the size and profitability of the reforestation and restoration program, compared to environmental education. Reforestation and restoration had been the initial program of the organization, and the environmental education program hadn't started until the organization was more than ten years old. Board members still related to the organization as a restoration organization and were surprised to see not only that more resources were going toward environmental education but also that the key program—in their minds—had a huge financial loss. The second revelation came around the nursery. Board members had started the nursery as an earned-revenue strategy to generate surpluses that could help support other initiatives. They were surprised to see that when the full costs were determined, the nursery didn't make money but actually was being subsidized by fundraising.

Now, looking at the Matrix Map, board and staff members alike can see and discuss their organization's programs and activities. Oftentimes the placement of activities along the impact and profitability axes can lead to good discussions about how programs are perceived in comparison to each other and about how we are accounting for our revenue and expenses. Shared understanding and discussion help lead to better decision making in the future. Even if the map shows an organization that looks sustainable today, we know that the world is constantly changing, and that what is sustainable today may not be tomorrow.

WHAT DOES IT MEAN WHEN A SECONDARY PROGRAM IS ACTUALLY BIGGER THAN OUR CORE PROGRAM?

A common realization that comes from looking at a Matrix Map is that a secondary program is larger financially, or even of higher impact, than what the board (or the staff) is used to thinking of as the core programs, the most important ones. This kind of insight occurs in other sectors as well. For example, some airports realize that they make more revenue from airport parking than they do from actual airport operations, but it would be illogical for them to shut down the airport operations and just keep the parking. The business lines of any business, for-profit or nonprofit, all work together.

At Everest Environmentalists, the realization that the environmental education program has grown so much can spark an important discussion. Does this growth represent changing public priorities, or has it been driven by staff seeing it as a priority? Should the board spend more time understanding the education program than it has typically done?

WHAT IF ALL OUR PROGRAMS ARE OF EQUALLY HIGH IMPACT?

The *Aha!* moment concerning programs of different relative sizes is so common that a word about it is important at this point. Just as organizations often find that the same or nearly the same impact score applies to clusters of programs, they also commonly find that all their programs rate highly on mission impact.

There can be many reasons why your programs all score high. People may be reluctant to seem critical of any program. People may be evaluating programs on the basis of their potential, not in terms of how they are actually delivered. The group of people you surveyed may have been nervous that their impressions might be made public and would offend someone. Or all your programs really may be excellent!

If all programs are rated high on mission impact, the easiest solution is to zoom in closer and examine *relative* impacts. In some instances, organizations must focus on fewer programs as they move toward sustainability. In these cases, a difference in impact, even if it is relatively minor, may be important.

Figures 6.13 and 6.14 show two views of the same human services organization. In the upper left quadrant of Figure 6.13 we see programs that have high impact but low profitability, and in the lower right quadrant of the figure we see programs that have low impact and high profitability. The current Matrix Map shows an unsustainable organization with too many activities that are losing money. Nevertheless, it is hard to differentiate among the activities because they all appear to have a similar impact. When we magnify the map, however, as we've done in Figure 6.14, you can begin to see some differentiation, albeit minor, among the various activities. These differences may become more relevant to the organization as it makes decisions with an orientation of sustainability. The differences can also form the starting point for a candid discussion among board and staff members, a discussion that may reveal even greater differences.

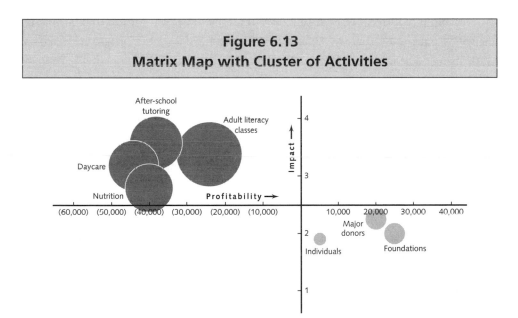

Figure 6.13
Matrix Map with Cluster of Activities

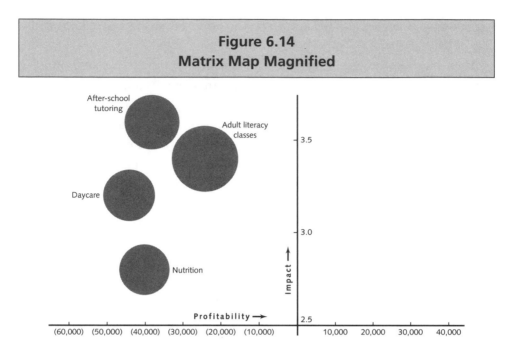

Figure 6.14
Matrix Map Magnified

There are two common, opposite reactions that people tend to have after looking at the Matrix Map of their organization. On the one hand, some people see unprofitable programs as simply needing to be axed. A program that is "losing money" is a program that is, in effect, being subsidized by other programs (such as fundraising) that make net financial contributions or contribute profitable earned income. An unrecognized assumption shared by many board and staff members may be that all programs should break even. Regardless of whether that assumption has been made explicit, the Matrix Map clearly shows which programs or business lines are losing money, and so it's only natural that some people will call for such programs to be cut. On the other hand, those who view an unprofitable program as crucially important may find themselves on the defensive. Often the least profitable programs are those for which the organization was founded, and with which it is now identified.

For instance, Everest Environmentalists began as a tree planting organization. The organization's Matrix Map showed the degree to which Everest's largest current programs are actually educational programs and local advocacy, both of which have defined, restricted funding streams. Some feel that keeping the tree planting program means holding unrealistically to the past. Why not let commercial services plant trees? But tree planting is more than just an important service—it is important to the organization's identity and meaning. For many, cutting that program is unthinkable.

Creating a Matrix Map in Microsoft Excel

Good news! It's easy to create a Matrix Map in Microsoft Excel or another spreadsheet software program. The details of the procedure will vary somewhat, depending on the particular software and version you're using, but the basic sequence of steps is the same. This example uses the steps available in Excel.

You start by creating a worksheet with four columns that contain the following information:

- The name of the program/business line
- The program/business line's net profit or loss (that is, the program/business line's surplus or deficit)
- The program/business line's mission impact rating
- The program/business line's expense total (the program/business line's total expenses as the measure for scale and size)

Then you enter your data under the appropriate rows. Your worksheet will look something like this:

	A	B	C	D
1	Name of Program/ Business Line	Net Profit/ Loss of Program/ Business Line	Mission Impact of Program/ Business Line	Expense Total of Program/ Business Line
2	Program A	(38,000)	4	180,000
3	Program B	85,000	3	740,000
4	Program C	(129,000)	4	2,111,000
5	Fundraiser X	145,000	2	92,000
6	Earned revenue Y	42,000	2	141,000

To create your Matrix Map, in most cases, you will need to select the data you've entered and then click either Chart Wizard or Insert Chart and follow your software's instructions for creating what Excel calls a *bubble chart*.* If you are familiar with creating charts in Excel, creating this type of chart will not be difficult. More detailed instructions specific to particular software versions can often be found online.

*Some very old versions of the software may not offer a bubble chart as one of the options, and some may create two bubbles for each program, in which case you will need to go to Chart Data Source and eliminate one of the series. Depending on the version of your software, you may need to make other adjustments as well (for example, the scale of one of the axes may need to be lengthened or shortened).

SUMMARY

After you have determined the profitability and impact for each activity in your organization, there are three steps for you to take in order to see your business model represented on the Matrix Map:

- Plot each activity as a circle on the Matrix Map, using profitability as the horizontal axis and impact as the vertical axis.

- Differentiate your activities by giving the circles on your map different degrees of shading. The activities shown on the Matrix Maps in this book are in shades of gray, but you may want to use colors for your circles, with different colors assigned to different programs according to their functions (blue for program activities, for example, or green for fundraising activities).

- Size the circles according to the expenses incurred by the activities. By doing so, you'll be able to see where the resources of each program are allocated.

The Matrix Map provides a visual image of the organization's business model. Upon seeing it, board and staff members will immediately be able to engage more adeptly in discussions about the organization's financial and programmatic sustainability and make better decisions aimed at improving the organization's position.

PART THREE Making Choices to Adjust the Business Model

In Part Two, we introduced the Matrix Map, a visual representation of the organization's business model. The Matrix Map, comprising all the organization's business lines, demonstrates how the organization's activities work together to create an organization that has programmatic impact and financial viability. But is the business model sustainable?

In Part Three, we discuss how you can use the Matrix Map to increase your organization's sustainability. We not only showcase the strategic imperatives for each business line, depending on where it is on the map (Chapter Seven), but also discuss how you can address some counterpoints that will inevitably arise when you are making decisions (Chapter Eight). We also discuss (Chapter Nine) how the map typically changes over time.

The Strategic Imperatives

The Matrix Map is a powerful tool for helping a nonprofit's board members and leaders understand and get a picture of the organization's business model. And, as with any other kind of picture, different people can read different things into it. But the Matrix Map can do more than just provide a snapshot of your situation. The Matrix Map directs users to strategies based on analysis of the organization's core activities, and it provides decision-making guidance as the organization strives for sustainability.

Getting to Nonprofit Sustainability

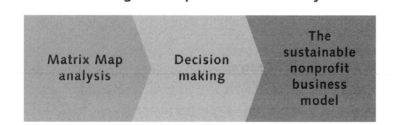

Strategic imperatives are the directions and actions that are called for by a program's placement on the Matrix Map. They represent a type of forced-choice model as a way of making decisions more rigorous.

In a forced-choice model, an action or decision is suggested by the analysis. It isn't necessary, of course, to make the choice to which the analysis points. But if the strategic imperative is rejected, it's important to have strong, compelling reasons why a different choice is being made.

Another advantage of a forced-choice model is that it prevents a group's making a decision by *not* making a decision. In cases where there are trade-offs and judgment calls to be made, it can be easy to allow decision making to drag on. When it feels as if a group just hasn't made a decision, often what's effectively true is that a poor decision has been made. For instance, a management team considers layoffs and their trade-offs, and it delays the decision several times while awaiting new information. In effect, the team has made the decision not to lay people off. That may have been the right choice, but in this instance it was made by default, without intentional, explicit choices on the part of leaders.

THE REASONS FOR STRATEGIC IMPERATIVES

The addition of strategic imperatives to the Matrix Map provides common ground for discussing the choices that face the activities in each quadrant of the map. Again, an organization is not obligated to adopt the suggested strategic imperative, but the imperative's very presence forces people to think clearly about why they might not take that path.

Researchers have revealed many obstacles to creative and effective group decision making. Here are a few:

- Individual and group bias toward the status quo
- The tendency of individuals to weight more for things that are vivid to them
- The tendency of individuals to weight shared information more heavily than information that is more the purview of one person or of a few people in the group

An important way of "unfreezing" a discussion is to introduce choices. We can look at an unimportant decision as a way of understanding this. Imagine that you have had the same framed poster on your kitchen wall for some time. If asked whether you like having the poster there, you might answer, "Yes, it's fine." But suppose someone brings you a new framed poster and asks, "Which poster would you rather have up in the kitchen?" The introduction of a new choice awakens your evaluative judgment. You look at the old poster with fresh eyes: What's good about it, and what's not? In the same way, the introduction of a forced choice, with a new alternative, is a powerful way of getting us to awaken our judgment.

STRATEGIC IMPERATIVES FOR EACH TYPE OF PROGRAM OR REVENUE ACTIVITY

Let's look carefully at each quadrant of the Matrix Map and at the strategic imperative for each one.

The Star: High Impact, High Profitability

Recall the Matrix Map for Midtown Multiservice Center (Figure 7.1), showing six core activities, including a significant Head Start preschool. By many measures, the Head Start preschool came out as an activity with high impact and high profitability. Staffed by highly talented, highly committed staff, the Head Start preschool makes a difference for children and their parents, in many ways. Anyone visiting the program can see the engagement and care of the staff, and the involvement of the parents as they come to pick up their children. Nationally, Head Start has also been the subject of many evaluations that have testified to the effectiveness of its model.

In addition, the Head Start preschool is well funded by the state (using federal funds), and the county also supports the program by funding various renovations and equipment purchases. Within Midtown Multiservice Center, the Head Start preschool obtains not only its full direct costs but also a fair share of administrative costs, and the building improvements constitute de facto support of all the programs. In short, the Head Start preschool has high impact and high profitability. We call programs like this one Stars (see Figure 7.2).

High-performing, well-funded programs in many organizations are led by high-performing staff directors. Such leaders often come from the line staff of these programs, and they know the programs well. These leaders are often

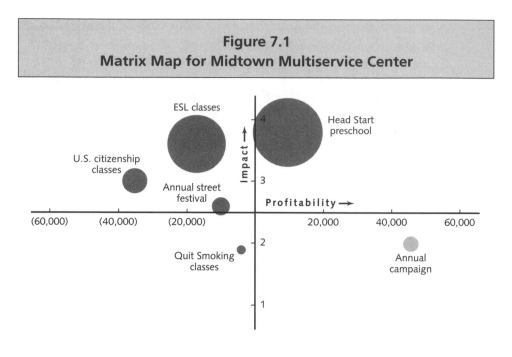

Figure 7.1
Matrix Map for Midtown Multiservice Center

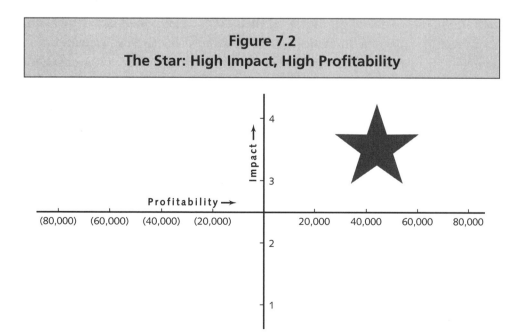

Figure 7.2
The Star: High Impact, High Profitability

self-directing and committed to excellence, and they work well with their programs' staff members and teams. To executive directors and boards, it seems as if such programs run themselves.

And that, of course, is the temptation—to let such a program run itself. At Midtown, the staff leaders and the board naturally turned their attention to the organization's underperforming activities. They sought to strengthen the weak programs and obtain more funding for them so they could increase staff and quality.

Each of the organization's activities has its own merits as it works to fulfill the organization's mission. But Midtown's leaders, without thinking through the strategic choices, and almost without noticing, were investing their scarcest, most precious resource—their focused attention—in another program, the one with the lowest impact and the lowest profitability, and they were neglecting their Star.

The strategic imperative for Stars is to invest in them and grow them (see Figure 7.3). In other words, the strategic imperative for a Star program is to do the opposite of taking it for granted while focusing on other, problematic areas.

Managers, of course, instinctively turn to problems and act to solve them. It's a positive characteristic, but it can lead those in charge of multiple programs to

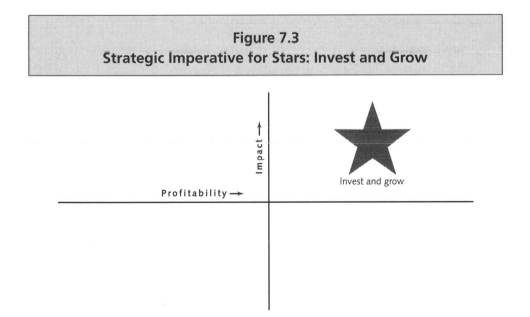

Figure 7.3
Strategic Imperative for Stars: Invest and Grow

turn their attention away from high-performing programs. The natural tendency is to try to strengthen the weaker programs, but in the process a high-performing program may be taken for granted.

But the fact is that Star programs, which have high impact both in the community and on the organization's strength, are the ones that are key to strategic growth. They are also the programs with the most potential, and as such they warrant investment not just of funds but also of senior management's attention.

Investment in a Star can take the form of time, attention, or money spent to gain a better understanding of your constituents' needs and of the services that other organizations are providing, not only in your local area but also in other cities. The organization may come up with innovations aimed at maintaining and increasing the Star's impact over time, and in the midst of inevitable change. For example, *investment* may take the following forms:

- Sending staff from a domestic violence shelter to another city to visit shelters there
- Testing an innovative idea, either with a planning/pilot grant or with the organization's own time and money
- Holding a retreat for the staff of a particular program and looking for internal challenges and suggestions for improvement from the people who understand the program firsthand
- Bringing together four or five experts in the field of a particular program, giving them a packet ahead of time, and then having them act as a panel in a half-day session with staff, where questions can be presented and the panel can be asked to consider them

Each of these examples demonstrates an investment of both time and money, with the aim of not only maintaining the activity's position as a Star but also recognizing its importance and growing the program.

The Stop Sign: Low Impact, Low Profitability

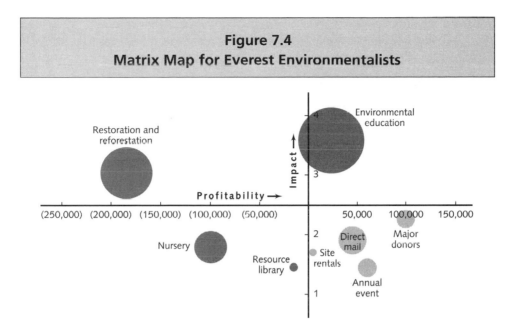

Figure 7.4
Matrix Map for Everest Environmentalists

At Everest Environmentalists (recall the organization's Matrix Map, shown again here in Figure 7.4), one of the rooms has been turned into a resource library. It has comfortable tables and chairs, and it's stocked with old books and handbooks on conservation and recycling. One more feature—it is empty. The original idea was that volunteers would drop in and enjoy the library, perhaps while waiting for their teams to go out on a clean-up crew. But most volunteers no longer meet at the ecology center. They are told their locations by e-mail and texting, and they meet at the worksites. The volunteers who do come in aren't interested in reading the faded books or the old magazines.

This resource library is a Stop Sign (Figure 7.5). It has low impact because it is seldom used. It has low profitability—it doesn't cost much, other than the space it uses, but it does use up that space. When managers think about the library, a natural instinct is to improve it. They consider buying computers for the library so that visitors can use them to read online materials and do research.

They decide to upgrade the publications. In other words, they invest in the lowest-impact, lowest-profitability program, out of an instinctive desire to help what is weak.

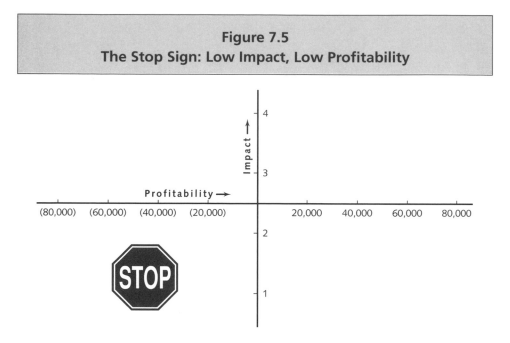

Figure 7.5
The Stop Sign: Low Impact, Low Profitability

The natural tendency is to try to improve a weak program. Instead, such a program should be closed down or given away. And that is the strategic imperative for a Stop Sign—to close it down or give it away (that is, divest from it rather than invest in it; see Figure 7.6). Here again, the strategic imperative shines through, forcing the discipline of confronting a stale program and making a proactive, thoughtful decision about what to do with it.

Everest Environmentalists should close down its resource library or consider donating the books to another organization. Perhaps, for instance, a computer can be moved to the lobby for visitors to use, and the library can be turned into a storage room. Perhaps the local public library can be convinced to have a "nonprofit shelf" where the books will go.

For the typical Stop Sign, there is usually a history of well-intentioned but ineffective efforts to turn the program around and make significant, lasting improvements. This effort may show up, for example, in the expansion of a newsletter that has been given a more professional appearance, or in the movement of the peer-learning roundtables, which have had fewer and fewer participants, from a midafternoon slot to a morning time, with breakfast included. In the case of Everest Environmentalists, is it possible to revitalize the resource

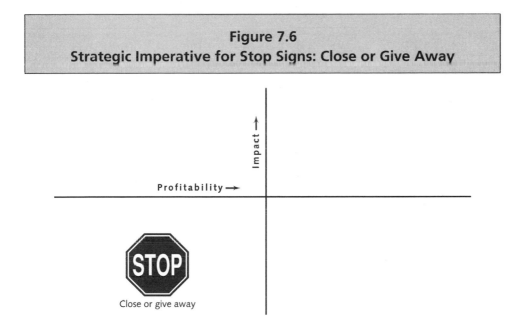

Figure 7.6
Strategic Imperative for Stop Signs: Close or Give Away

Impact →

Profitability →

STOP

Close or give away

library and make it a vibrant community meeting place? Maybe. It may well be worth one last push, with a cost ceiling and a deadline.

Management needs to assess the costs and possible benefits of investing in a Stop Sign. Perhaps a plan for Everest Environmentalists will be developed that involves $4,000 for a new computer and books and a publicity campaign, with the goal of having at least ten volunteers per day use the resource library. The questions here, among others, are whether the investment will bring more volunteers to use the library, and, if it does, whether their increased use of the library actually is worth the organization's investment of money and time. For a discussion of the impact on common and administrative costs when a program is shut down, see Exhibit 7.1.

Sometimes it just doesn't occur to an organization that activities can be stopped, that programs can be shut down, and that a fundraiser can be discontinued. One executive director commented, "I've been telling our development staff that they just have to get the volunteers for the pancake breakfast. One day the development director said, 'It's a huge amount of work, and we hardly make any money off it anymore. Why don't we just stop doing it?' It was a revelation to both of us."

Exhibit 7.1. Closing a Program: Impact on Common and Administrative Costs

Closing a program is seldom an easy task for an organization because of the emotional connection that constituents, board members, and staff often feel with their programs. Financially, it may appear that a program is losing money, and only later is it discovered, after the program has been closed, that the expected gain has not been realized. This discovery can lead to infighting as well as to distrust of information and analysis in the future. Therefore, we need to make sure that we fully understand the numbers that stand behind our decision making.

When we determine the profitability of a business line, we consider the full cost of that business line, including its direct costs (such as costs incurred for program staff and supplies specifically for that program). We also consider that business line's portion of costs that are common and shared between multiple business lines (such as occupancy costs, costs for technology), and the business line's portion of administrative expenses (such as the time of the accounting staff). Together, all these costs are the ones required to operate the business line.

Therefore, when a business line closes, the only costs that directly go away are its direct costs. Let's say, for example, that a food bank decides to shut down its nutrition education program. The organization eliminates the two educators who were on staff, thus also eliminating reimbursement for their travel and for the printing of the curriculum. Typically, however, the technology department won't lay off 10 percent of its two-person staff, and the organization is not able to reduce its rent or the cost of its liability insurance. Instead, these shared costs are just shifted to other programs in the organization.

When we assess the financial gain that we hope to see from shutting a business line, we should think of the potential savings only in terms of the program's direct expenses. In the for-profit sector, a business line is typically kept open as long as it is covering its direct expenses because any contribution toward overhead is recognized as helpful. The same approach can sometimes be taken in the nonprofit sector. Here are some questions and ideas to consider if you are looking at shutting a program down:

- Does the allocated revenue cover the direct expenses? If it does, you should look at the common and administrative costs.

- If you eliminate this business line, will you reduce your common or administrative costs at all? Sometimes there may be savings in terms of costs for occupancy, insurance, technology, and maybe even the accounting staff. These expenses are more difficult to reduce, but it can be done.

- What will be the effect of shifting the business line's common and administrative expenses to other business lines? How will that decision affect those business lines' profitability? Even if you eliminate a business line that is losing money, shifting the burden of the closed program's administrative and common costs may still leave your organization in a position that is not financially sustainable. Your finance staff should be able to demonstrate what the impact of these changes will be and help you determine whether shutting the business line down will help your sustainability.

The Heart: High Impact, Low Profitability

At Midtown Multiservice Center (see Figure 7.1), the ESL classes started out being delivered to a small group of immigrant community members who had expressed interest. After word spread that the program was being offered, interest grew, and the number of classes being offered increased. The center developed a sliding scale fee schedule, which charged a higher fee to those who could more ably afford the classes. The reality, however, is that the majority of the classes' clients were at the low end of the sliding scale, paying almost nothing. Those who could afford the classes were taking them at the local community college or buying books and tapes and learning on their own.

As the program grew, what had started out small, requiring a subsidy of only $3,000 per year, grew to the point where it was losing close to $17,000 per year. The program may continue in its current state for many years, but eventually one of two things will probably happen—either more people will come, which will mean a bigger program and an even larger subsidy, or tough economic times will reduce the donations and fundraising that were, in effect, subsidizing the program, and its continuation may mean financial hardship for the organization.

In such a context, staff and board members often see their choices as two polar opposites—close it, or keep it but try to raise more money. The debate gets framed as one in which being fiscally responsible is pitted against serving a low-income community. This debate is not only unwinnable through analysis but also unnecessary.

Ian McMillan has characterized programs that are high in impact and low in profitability as "soul of the agency" programs. On the Matrix Map, we call these programs Hearts (see Figure 7.7).

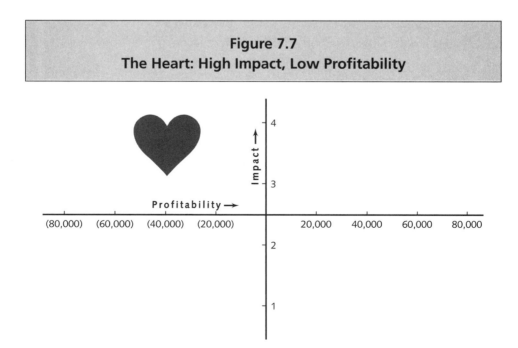

Figure 7.7
The Heart: High Impact, Low Profitability

For Midtown Multiservice Center, the reason why the ESL classes have high impact is that ESL classes are not available elsewhere at such a low price. The ESL program enables communication and therefore builds community—the core of the organization's mission. Rather than decide to ax the program or simply raise more money—unlikely in the current environment—the board decided to keep it but limit its size. It was recognized that even though there was growing demand for the program, it would be limited. The program would continue with its sliding scale, but the net loss could be no more than $12,000. In keeping with this new goal, either classes would have to become larger or the organization would have to start a waiting list for future classes.

The strategic imperative for a Heart is to keep it but control its costs (Figure 7.8). Hearts cannot be allowed to drive the organization into bankruptcy.

In a human services organization, controlling costs may mean reducing the level of service or limiting the number of people who can be served. For instance, a drop-in center might reduce its hours, or an after-school engineering program might limit the number of students it can accept. An environmental organization might sharply cut back on its youth camping programs—again, keeping the

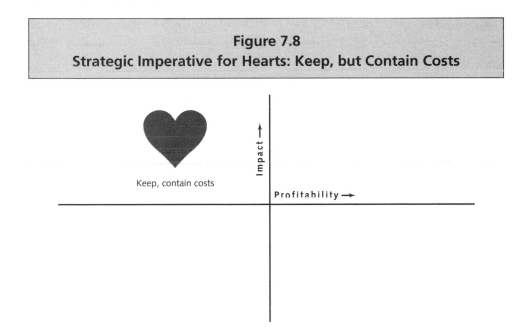

Figure 7.8
Strategic Imperative for Hearts: Keep, but Contain Costs

Heart, but setting limits on the degree to which the organization can subsidize the activity with its unrestricted funds.

It's frequently a temptation to look at a cherished, highly subsidized program and say, "Let's just raise money for it." Sometimes this is an appropriate strategy, and an organization can choose in such a case not to limit the program's costs (at least not right away) but to limit new investments of time and money. For example, an organization may choose to devote significant senior staff time to raising money for its youth camping programs but set a limit of three months before revisiting the question of whether the program can be maintained at its original level.

Another way to think about a Heart is to say, "We want two Hearts, and we can afford two Hearts. But we can't have thirty Hearts." The organization may be able to subsidize some Hearts, but too many Hearts make an organization unsustainable.

Discussions about Heart programs often involve the belief that such programs generate indirect income. For instance, someone might argue that some major donors to the organization are chiefly moved by a program that is a Heart, or that a Heart program is what enables another program to be a Star. In these cases, the strategic imperative still holds.

For example, take a housing development organization that builds and manages housing for low-income families. The organization has been very successful at navigating its way through the complicated mix of government regulation, commercial lenders, nonprofit lenders, NIMBY (Not In My Back Yard) politics, and construction contractors' rules and practices. The organization also provides residents with supportive services, such as family counseling, assistance enrolling in job training, programs to combat substance abuse, and so forth. Nevertheless, even though there is funding for these supportive services, their delivery costs more than the funding allows. In short, these activities are Hearts—they are unprofitable, but their impact is high.

The organization's management has made the argument that although the supportive services lose money, they excite great interest and sympathy from the broader community, and they bring political support as well as support against NIMBY efforts. Management sees the supportive services not only as effective for residents but also as crucial to maintaining the political and community support that allows the housing development side of the organization to be successful.

In this instance, the impact of the supportive services would be raised because they not only have an impact on the community but also have an impact on the ability of other activities to deliver their own services and have their own impact. Again, though, the strategic imperative would be to keep the supportive services but control their costs. It might be possible to double the number of contracts and the number of people helped by the supportive services, but doing so would probably double the deficit as well. Service responsibility and fiscal responsibility can be balanced in an intentional, quantitative way that serves the community and also helps out the policy programs.

The Money Tree: Low Impact, High Profitability

The opposite of the high-impact, low-profitability Heart is the low-impact, high-profitability Money Tree (see Figure 7.9).

Some activities may be viewed as having little mission impact but being profitable. Such fundraisers typically raise a substantial amount of money, but staff often

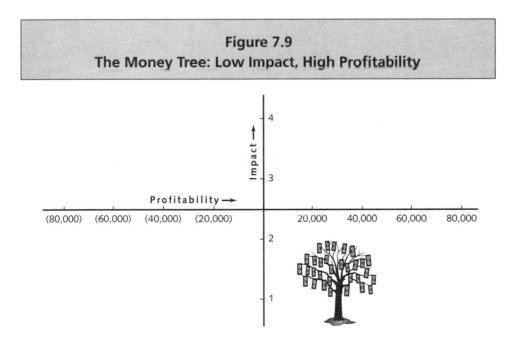

Figure 7.9
The Money Tree: Low Impact, High Profitability

question their importance. For example, someone may ask sarcastically, "Are we in the business of putting on parties for rich people or helping poor people?"

The strategic imperative for a Money Tree is to keep it, increase its impact, and make sure it is nurtured. Money Trees require care. Just like regular trees, they need to be watered and attended to (see Figure 7.10).

Just as Hearts and Stars play an important role in an organization, so do Money Trees. Their resources subsidize Hearts, and when we have the orientation of sustainability, we value activities for their contributions to both impact and profitability.

One uninformed reaction to an activity's being characterized as a Money Tree is to neglect it as much as possible while still wanting it to continue generating money. When this occurs, some staff and board members may disdain an event as not being mission-driven, and the executive director, the fundraising staff, and the fundraising board members may feel that they are being looked down on. But the opposite reaction can also occur: "We're making so much on this luncheon, maybe we should have a dinner, too!" Although Money Trees are important, however, it may not be appropriate to invest in another ten that are similar.

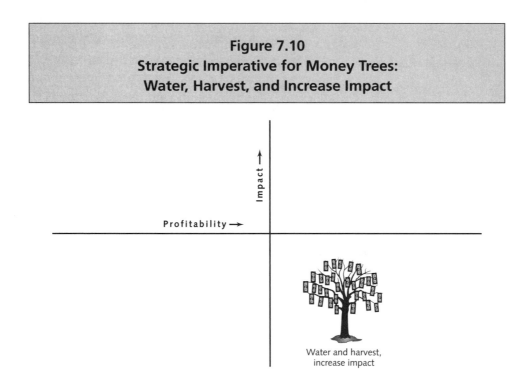

Figure 7.10
Strategic Imperative for Money Trees:
Water, Harvest, and Increase Impact

Impact →

Profitability →

Water and harvest,
increase impact

Money Trees must be watered and cared for. Donors must be thanked. Special events must be constantly refreshed, and marketing materials must be updated and redesigned. We must be responsible and artful in the care of our orchards. But we can do even more.

When we think of fundraising activities, we are often so focused on the money they will generate that we sometimes don't think of them in terms of their mission impact. The strategic imperative of the Money Tree—keep it and increase its impact—forces us to look at this role of the activity.

Each year, for example, Tempest Theater sends its donors and friends a beautifully designed invitation to a special reception and fundraising event. Board members send this invitation to their own friends, and one friend of a board member called to say, "I've never heard of this theater. What's the point of them?"

Invitations are more than vehicles for getting people to attend an event. They are a kind of mini-educational program in themselves. In fact, many more people will participate in the "invitation program" than in the event itself. One way to increase the impact of this Money Tree is to make use of the invitation to increase impact. Next year, for example, the nicely designed invitation can also include a photo and a short, compelling paragraph about the importance of Tempest Theater's after-school drama workshops.

To reiterate, the strategic imperative for a Money Tree is to keep it, water it (but think hard before buying any more), and enhance its impact.

A Quick Matrix Map Without Quantitative Analysis

Can the Matrix Map be used in a group setting without quantitative analysis? Here is a Matrix Map that was developed in about thirty minutes at a meeting of board and staff members who were looking at four of their organization's nine annual special events. This organization wanted to cut back on the number of its special events. At the same time, however, the board and staff members realized that each of the events made money and was quite well attended. There were volunteers working on every one, and there were volunteers who attended and enjoyed them all.

(Continued)

The group started by listing the four events down the left-hand column and quickly moved on to decide each event's impact level, its profitability level, and the level of effort it required. After a quick, near-consensus discussion, each event was assigned to a program type—Heart, Star, Stop Sign, or Money Tree—and then the appropriate strategic imperatives were discussed. The illustration of this group's fast analysis shows impact ratings as well as what the board and staff members ultimately decided to do about four of the events.

Event	Impact	Profit	Effort	Type	Action
Senior lunch	High	Low	Medium	♥	Keep, contain costs
Crab feed	Medium	Medium but growing	High	★	Grow, increase impact
New Year's event	Low	Low	High	STOP	Give to church that also has one
Autumn festival	Low	High	High	(money tree)	Grow, increase impact

A FINAL WORD ON STRATEGIC IMPERATIVES

The strategic imperatives for each quadrant of the Matrix Map are the choices that sustainability *demands* (see Figure 7.11). The sustainable nonprofit business model does not come from the unknown. It comes from a hard look at the current, de facto business model, and then from an intelligent consideration of the strategic imperatives. The adjustments to the business model that the strategic imperatives detail, taken together, result in the sustainable nonprofit business model.

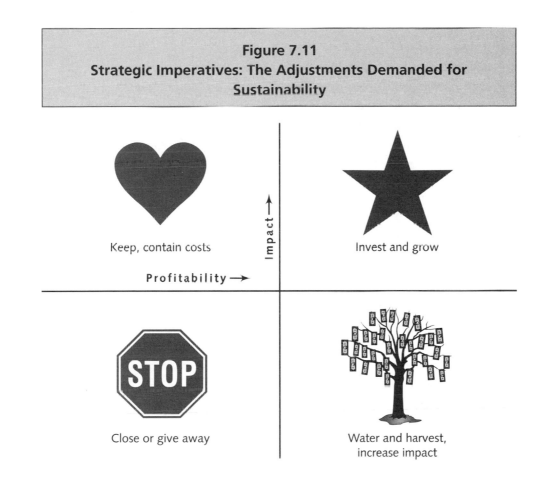

Figure 7.11
Strategic Imperatives: The Adjustments Demanded for Sustainability

Impact →

Profitability →

Keep, contain costs

Invest and grow

Close or give away

Water and harvest, increase impact

Mapping Fundraising Activities

The examples we have shown until now have all centered on organizational mapping of business lines, an exercise that includes programmatic as well as development activities. Depending on the question that is being asked, however, an organization may map only some of its business lines—just the ones for which information is needed to make a strategic decision. If an organization is considering adding another event or development activity, it may map the relevant business line as a way of assessing the relative impact of the proposed event or activity and making

(Continued)

The Strategic Imperatives   **93**

a decision about it. In a case where we map only development-oriented business lines, we may change the criteria by which we evaluate impact.

For example, consider an art museum that is trying to pare down the number of its fundraising events. Leaders decide to use the Matrix Map in their effort, and a task force comes up with criteria by which to evaluate the impact of the museum's current activities. Here are some possible criteria:

- *Cultivation:* How good a job does the event do at cultivating potential new members or upgrading current members?

- *Alignment with mission:* Does the event educate members about art in a way that is aligned with our mission?

- *Publicity:* Will the event enhance the museum's image or raise awareness of the museum in the community?

- *Competition:* Is the event unique in the city, or are there several similar types of events?

After evaluating all its existing events on the criteria listed, the organization created the Matrix Map shown in the following illustration.

An initial glance at the map shows the number of events that the art museum already holds. Clearly, it holds some events (such as tours, lectures, and receptions with artists) that further the mission of the organization but do not make money. However, these events may help support the membership drive, the President's Circle, and unrestricted fundraising. By contrast, the event called Wine & Art neither makes money nor has a high impact. This event looks like a probable candidate for elimination. The auction and the gala dinner each score low on impact, but both are profitable. Events like these often lead to struggles with the development committee because some people argue that these should be more mission-focused. Perhaps they should, although the Matrix Map also shows the importance of these events in generating resources. It would seem from this analysis that the development department does have a good number of mission-oriented events, and that the primary focus of the auction and the gala dinner should be to raise money. Remember, a Money Tree is a valuable element of an organization that is oriented toward sustainability!

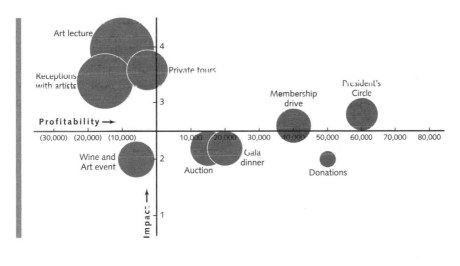

SUMMARY

For each quadrant of the Matrix Map there are certain strategic imperatives that help guide the choices for the organization's business activities.

High-impact, low-profitability activities are called Hearts, and the strategic imperative is to keep these activities and maintain their impact but contain their costs while you explore alternative revenue strategies. Hearts are very important to organizations, but too many Hearts can quickly make an organization unsustainable.

Activities that are high on both impact and profitability are called Stars. Here, the imperative is for these activities to be invested in and grown. Too often the fate of these activities is left to chance as the staff and the board focus on bigger challenges, but that is just the opposite of what should happen.

Activities that are highly profitable but low on impact are called Money Trees and typically consist of fundraising activities. These activities should be continued, with the focus on increasing their impact while maintaining their profitability.

Activities that are unprofitable and have low impact are called Stop Signs. These activities may have been important to the organization at one time, and they may still be important to the community, but there are other efforts that have more value to the organization. The strategic imperative here is to discontinue these activities and perhaps let them be carried out by another organization.

Toward the New Business Model

The Matrix Map shows the organization's business model and provides strategic imperatives that will lead to sustainability, but acts of decision making and implementation are what ultimately create a sustainable organization. Given how much time managers spend making decisions, most have relatively few structures available to them as they structure decision processes. In this chapter, we'll analyze the Matrix Maps for each of our archetypal organizations and walk through the decision-making process undertaken by one of them, Everest Environmentalists.

EVEREST ENVIRONMENTALISTS

The Matrix Map for Everest Environmentalists, as discussed in Chapters Six and Seven, is shown again here in Figure 8.1. The board of directors' initial reactions to the map ranged from surprise to the realization that environmental education was now the organization's largest program, and that it was now larger than the restoration and reforestation program that had started the organization. In addition, the board was surprised that the organization's plant nursery was actually losing money. That program had been started for the primary purpose of generating profits to subsidize the restoration work. The strategic imperatives for each of the organization's activities are shown in Table 8.1.

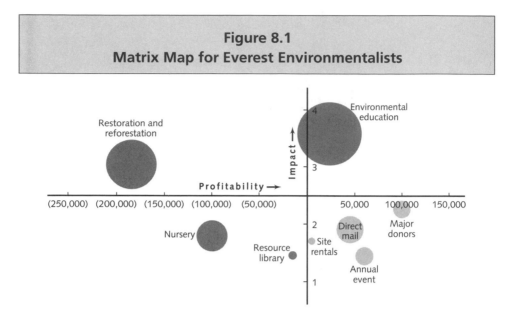

Figure 8.1

Matrix Map for Everest Environmentalists

TABLE 8.1
Strategic Imperatives for Everest Environmentalists

Core Activity	Matrix Map Quadrant	Strategic Imperative
Environmental education	Star	Invest and grow
Restoration and reforestation	Heart	Keep, and contain costs
Nursery	Stop Sign	Close or divest
Resource library	Stop Sign	Close or divest
Solicitation of major donors	Money Tree	Increase impact
Site rentals	Money Tree	Increase impact
Annual event	Money Tree	Increase impact
Direct mail	Money Tree	Increase impact

Generative and Creative Thinking for Strategic Alternatives

Although the strategic imperatives may be clear, the process for making decisions often involves some strategic and creative thinking. For example, the strategic imperative for the nursery is to close it down. The nursery is not having a significant impact and is being subsidized. But the implementation of that imperative requires more thought. Should it simply be closed down? If so, what about the existing inventory and the equipment? What about the volunteers who grow native plants for the nursery? Should the organization see whether the nursery program can be transferred to another organization? If so, would that mean losing the nursery volunteers to that organization?

Once the strategic imperative is realized, it is important to articulate what success will look like in the imperative's execution. This may seem like an obvious step, but it's helpful to articulate what we want to achieve through appropriate implementation. For Everest Environmentalists, success would have two basic elements—to reduce the nursery's negative financial impact to zero, and to avoid losing volunteers who had become alienated or had simply moved on to another organization.

After defining what success will look like, the next step in our implementation is to generate alternatives that might meet these criteria. Several alternatives immediately occurred to the senior management team at Everest:

- Hold a meeting to explain to volunteers why the plant nursery is being discontinued, and allow them to take home any existing inventory
- Sell the remaining inventory to a commercial nursery, and use the proceeds to have a thank-you reception for nursery volunteers
- Approach a local gardening society to see if it would be willing to take over the plant nursery
- See if a community college's horticultural program would consider taking over the nursery

Most of these options would meet the stated goals while following the strategic imperatives and helping the organization become sustainable.

The Environment for Creativity

One way of sparking new ideas or coming up with creative solutions is to keep the options open a little longer than feels necessary. Nonprofits tend to spend relatively little time generating creative alternatives. In the process of generating ways to implement a strategic imperative, a nonprofit may hold a brainstorming session at which alternatives are generated, and then quite a bit of the management team's time will be devoted to agonizing over those alternatives. A parallel situation arises in hiring, where it's common to spend a great deal of time reviewing résumés, interviewing applicants, and making the hire but relatively little time and effort generating a strong applicant pool. The choice of where to put time and effort is usually made unconsciously.

In a generative strategy process, it's important to invest more time—even more than you might think is necessary—in generating creative, alternative ideas. In fact, one role that leaders play in decision making is to hold the organization's mind open just a little longer than others may think is necessary—the equivalent of holding the application process open a little longer so that more qualified applicants can be found before hiring managers move on to the selection process.

At Everest Environmentalists, it would have been easy to say, "Okay, now we have to decide which of these alternatives we're going to implement." But by thinking just a little longer—maybe even just an hour longer, or a day longer—managers are often forced to think more deeply, more creatively, more wildly, and more imaginatively.

Another technique to spark ideas is to bring staff members and decision makers into the heart of the area being discussed. An executive director who was hired to lead a multiprogram organization may not really understand the gestalt of a particular program. If decision makers visit the program area when the program is in operation, they may see something new or think in new ways about how the program operates. This process would be similar to what happens with the immersion technique in foreign-language learning. Someone can study a foreign language and culture for years, but spending a month in the country where the language is spoken will probably give that person a much more compelling, holistic feeling for the culture. In the case of Everest Environmentalists, the executive director spent five hours on a Saturday at the plant nursery. He helped with sales, but he also spent a couple of hours doing paperwork on his laptop computer a few yards to the side of the sales area. In other words, he hung around. When he noticed a volunteer moving a few gallon pots from the back of her car to the car of another volunteer, he asked what was going on, and the two volunteers sheepishly admitted that one of them was giving plants to the other without selling them through the plant nursery. The director assured them that this was fine. But the encounter gave him a new idea—maybe a plant-exchange program was a way to keep the nursery business line alive in a small way while continuing to provide an activity for volunteers. In this way, the organization could stop its financial losses on the nursery but keep the engagement of the nursery volunteers.

The final step before deciding how to implement an imperative is to hold all the options up against the impact and profitability criteria and decide which option is best. Odd as it may seem, many groups often generate alternatives but then fail to hold them up against the criteria. Leaders at Everest Environmentalists looked back at their criteria and combined several options to meet their goals. The final decision looked like this:

- Close the plant nursery and work out a relationship with a local nursery to take the existing inventory, with a portion of the proceeds from the sale going to support the organization.
- Hold a meeting with volunteers to announce the decision (and the thinking about the decision) as well as the new plant-exchange program.
- Operate the plant-exchange program out in the community, at the same sites where the restoration and reforestation initiatives are offered, to encourage volunteers to get involved in the organization's other activities.

What is important is that the organization made a decision, based on the strategic imperatives, to improve its sustainability and then implemented that decision in the best way possible. The decisions that came out of the Matrix Map process for Everest Environmentalists are shown in Table 8.2.

TABLE 8.2
Everest Environmentalists: Decisions Made on the Basis of Strategic Imperatives

Core Activity	Matrix Map Quadrant	Strategic Imperative	Decision Made
Environmental education	Star	Invest and grow	Review curriculum for relevance and other options for online learning
Restoration and reforestation	Heart	Keep, and contain costs	Limit reforestation initiatives to six per year
			Reduce losses to $100,000
			Explore new revenue strategies
Nursery	Stop Sign	Close or divest	Close down

(Continued)

Core Activity	Matrix Map Quadrant	Strategic Imperative	Decision Made
Resource library	Stop Sign	Close or divest	Divest to public library
Solicitation of major donors	Money Tree	Increase impact	Review materials for educational opportunities
Site rentals	Money Tree	Increase impact	Educate groups to be more environmentally friendly in their use of the facilities
Annual event	Money Tree	Increase impact	Create the annual event as a zero-waste event, and showcase it as an educational opportunity to reduce waste
Direct mail	Money Tree	Increase impact	Make topics more educational

TABLE 8.2 (Continued)

Why Are Organizations So Reluctant to Close Programs?

A homeless shelter decided to close its free clothing program. Factoring into the decision were the increased costs of sorting, cleaning, and storing donated clothing, the increased disposal costs for unsuitable clothing, and the presence of a nearby Salvation Army store. To an outside analyst, closing the program might have seemed like a no-brainer.

But it was a difficult decision for the organization. One of the board members had once been homeless himself, and at the meeting he talked about the comfort of clothes and shoes that were clean and new to him. Others pointed out that clothing donations were often donors' first contact with the organization, and they worried that refusing used clothing would turn donors off. Staff members pointed out that if overnight visitors could conveniently get free clean clothes, cleanliness within the shelter would be improved.

The clothing program was a Heart. It was close to the organization's mission, but because it served so few people, it couldn't be seen as a high-impact program, and because the draw it exerted on donors could not be quantified, the program wasn't placed at the lowest point on the profitability scale.

Like other tough decisions, this one was a judgment call. Not everyone was in agreement, and there were legitimate arguments on both sides.

The idea of closing the program felt like an erosion of the organization's mission and values, and there was concern over which program would be next to get the ax. Ultimately, a majority of the board voted to close the program and transfer it to the Salvation Army.

Was that the right decision? Again, it's a judgment call. We could debate for decades whether it was the right judgment call. Many alternatives had been raised, analyzed, and deemed infeasible. Unlike a for-profit company's decision to eliminate a minor product line, this decision called for judgments about mission impact, impact on donors and staff, costs, and symbolic value. The Matrix Map helped the organization decide that although the program was valuable, the organization's extremely limited money and time had to be invested elsewhere.

MIDTOWN MULTISERVICE CENTER

Midtown Multiservice Center's Matrix Map (seen again here in Figure 8.2) clearly demonstrated what Midtown's board members thought they knew—that the organization was operating in an unsustainable manner. But what to do? The strategic imperatives helped the organization restructure some of its programs and make some hard decisions (see Table 8.3).

Figure 8.2
Matrix Map for Midtown Multiservice Center

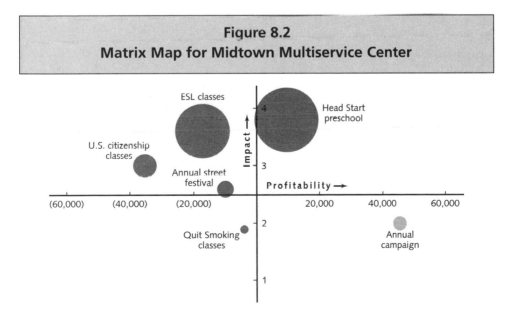

TABLE 8.3
Midtown Multiservice Center: Decisions Made on the Basis of Strategic Imperatives

Core Activity	Matrix Map Quadrant	Strategic Imperative	Decision Made
Head Start preschool	Star	Invest and grow	Market and try to grow Maintain government relations
ESL classes	Heart	Keep, and contain costs	Limit attendance Try a partnership with the local community college
U.S. citizenship classes	Heart	Keep, and contain costs	Increase class size and reduce number of classes
Annual street festival	Heart	Keep, and contain costs	Raise corporate sponsorship fees Contain budget
Quit Smoking classes	Stop Sign	Close or divest	Shut down, and refer people to other local organizations providing classes
Annual campaign	Money Tree	Increase impact	Make conscious effort to build larger mailing list Use a campaign to educate people on the demographics of the community

TEMPEST THEATER

At Tempest Theater, board members were pleasantly surprised to see that the after-school drama workshops they had been taking for granted were a Star. Tempest's Matrix Map (seen again here in Figure 8.3) also clearly pointed out the organization's Hearts, and the board took on the strategic imperative of deciding how to contain those programs' costs. The decisions that were made are shown in Table 8.4.

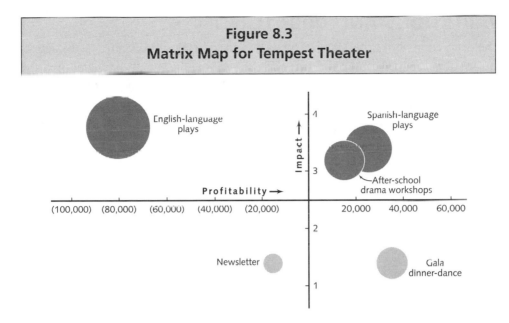

Figure 8.3
Matrix Map for Tempest Theater

TABLE 8.4			
Tempest Theater: Decisions Made on the Basis of Strategic Imperatives			
Core Activity	**Matrix Map Quadrant**	**Strategic Imperative**	**Decision Made**
Spanish-language plays	Star	Invest and grow	Consider adding more plays or more performances of each play
After-school drama workshops	Star	Invest and grow	Conduct a marketing campaign to increase enrollment
English language performances of plays originally in Spanish	Heart	Keep, and contain costs	Reduce the number of plays performed each year. Limit losses to $50,000
Newsletter	Stop Sign	Stop or divest	Since the newsletter drives attendance for shows, combine as a marketing expense into programs, and contain costs
Gala dinner-dance	Money Tree	Increase impact	Educate invitees more about the programs of the theater

VARIATIONS AND COUNTERPOINTS

The discussion about the Matrix Map is bound to bring out objections, disagreements, and arguments. All the better! Such disagreements are how the organization comes to a deeper understanding of the analysis that the Matrix Map provides, and thereby makes smarter decisions.

There are some counterpoints that are commonly raised in a Matrix Map discussion. Here are a few that drive variations on the strategic imperatives and open the organization to creativity and exciting new thinking.

The Loss Leader

"If we look at the free lunch-hour workshops we offer, it seems that they are losing money. But people go to those workshops and are so impressed with the presenter and our organization that they sign up for our $200 workshops on the same topic. If we get rid of the free workshops, we'll end up hurting our paid workshop program."

First, when it comes to loss leaders, we often make assumptions that haven't been reconfirmed in recent years. Consider doing a fast study to see how many people in the paid program have gone first to a free workshop. This study can be as simple as passing out short survey forms in paid workshops and asking participants whether they have attended a free workshop before a paid one, and if so, what the free one was about.

Second, if the free workshops actually are effective at enrolling paid participants, the free workshops need to be seen as belonging to the same program as the paid workshops. If the purpose of the free workshops is to drive enrollment in the paid workshops, then the free workshops are similar to advertising or outreach costs—they need to be included as costs of the workshop program.

One good choice for a loss leader, then, is to make it a part of the program it supports. The net effect will be to decrease the profitability of the workshop program as a whole but make the workshop managers more keenly attuned to ensuring that the free workshops really do drive paid enrollments.

The Pet Project

Some programs or events are nice but not compelling—except perhaps to one person. Sometimes that person is a major donor. Sometimes that person is an important board member. Sometimes that person is the executive director.

The Founders' Day dinner is such an event at Tempest Theater. A down-home meal is served, with homemade tamales, and monologues from past plays are performed. Originally the Founders' Day dinner was like a family reunion for early volunteers and staff. Then it became a cultivation event, and now it is sparsely attended. Staff members drag their feet putting it on, and they dread attending. But it's so meaningful to two of the founders—who are also major donors—that it's hard to contemplate closing this admittedly low-impact, low-profitability Stop Sign.

Although some people on the staff were eager to get rid of this Stop Sign, others had a tender spot for it. But even those with the most tender hearts couldn't make a compelling argument for the amount of staff time and energy that went into this event. Finally, somebody pondering the word *divest* thought of someone to whom the Founders' Day dinner could be given—the two founders. It was proposed that the organization contribute a set amount toward a catered dinner at the home of one of the founders, who would be responsible for invitations and hosting. There would be only one monologue, and the senior staff members and board officers would attend. The founders were pleased.

There may not always be a creative solution. For the board and staff members at Tempest Theater, however, having a strategic imperative staring them in the face—one they didn't like—made them come up with a creative decision that might not have been reached without the pressure of a forced-choice situation.

Keeping a Foot in the Door

Executive directors often see dozens of possible opportunities for the organization. It's like standing in a room with dozens of doors, some slightly open and some tightly closed. It's not possible to see past or through a door to tell whether the opportunity on the other side is small or great, nor is it possible to predict which doors will open wide by themselves and which will fail to open even after a lot of kicking.

Executive directors understandably want to keep a foot in each open door to keep it from closing. In this context, most Stop Sign programs look like small placeholders that need to be kept so that if a door opens more widely, the organization is poised to walk through it. In fact, one reason why executive directors are so overworked is that they want to keep the organization's feet in all these doors but can't justify the investment of organizational resources, and so they use their own after-hours time on this effort. (This is not to say that their time and energy are not organizational resources—they are, and very valuable ones at that).

Examples of such Stop Signs are the small, money-losing TB prevention program that an AIDS clinic keeps going because someday TB may be where the opportunities lie, or the money-losing radio program that a youth organization produces, even though no one listens to it, just in case funding and an audience materialize one day.

In addition to carrying out an analysis of the organization's Stop Signs, the organization's leaders will need to make judgment calls about whether these programs should be stopped or are instead moderately risky investments, a limited number of which should be maintained. Often the Matrix Map provides a basis for organizational discipline. The organization can't continue to maintain thirty moderately risky investments. The discipline of choosing which long-term long shots should be kept and which must be abandoned (at least for now) is an important aspect of strategic sustainability.

Keeping Others Out by Staking Your Claim to Territory

Sometimes more than one organization sees the same territory as its own service area, and all these organizations resent others coming in with similar services. For example, each of two neighboring cities may have a bicycle coalition. Coalition A is offering workshops on bike repair in a suburb that lies between the two cities. Usually this workshop is poorly attended, but staff members argue that keeping it holds the territory for Coalition A and prevents Coalition B from offering workshops in the same suburb.

The situation does not necessarily demand that Coalition A cancel its bike repair workshops in that suburb. There may be other reasons, apart from a particular program, why it is a good idea to keep potential competitors out of a geographical area, a program area, or an audience area. If that's the case, the program in question should be considered a marketing expense for the organization or for a program to be developed in the future.

People Need This Program but Don't Know It

Staff members at Everest Environmentalists often find themselves driven crazy by the sight of a recently planted tree that is suffering from mistreatment or neglect. The poor treatment could be coming at the hands of a property owner or resident, but often it comes at the hands of ill-informed paid gardeners employed by a household. Two years ago, Everest Environmentalists obtained a small grant to develop a free workshop on how to care for common street trees, and it was offered at some libraries and garden centers. Despite poor attendance, the staff believes strongly in these workshops as a vehicle not only for educating people about tree care but also for empowering them to be owners of the public spaces in their neighborhoods.

Even though it is a good program, there is no market for it. On its own, this activity may make sense, but the Matrix Map allows staff members to see the activity in the context of the entire organization. Everest Environmentalists cannot support another Heart. In fact, it isn't sustainable right now, and even though this program has impact, the impact of the restoration and reforestation program is greater. Heartbreaking though the fact may be, these are low-impact, low-profitability workshops. Time to stop them.

Why Don't We Just Raise Money for It?

A new executive director was told by the board and the staff, "There's a $300,000 hole in the budget that you have to fill." Not only is this a dishearteningly phrased directive, it's an unproductive way to characterize a financially difficult situation.

Behind this statement is the unspoken assumption that programs and their funding occupy two separate spheres rather than fitting into an overall business model for the organization. In addition, by overlooking the existence of a business model, the board and the staff lost the opportunity to *manage* the mission impact and financial strategies together.

There are many variations on the hope, often unrealistic, that unfettered money will simply come in from somewhere. To exaggerate slightly, there is scarcely a board in the United States where someone hasn't suggested that all the money problems will be solved if the organization approaches either Bill Gates or Oprah Winfrey.

The Matrix Map provides a framework for identifying activities where profitability can be increased as well as a conceptual foundation for analyzing new ideas. But it doesn't take the place of leadership. Leaders must seek creative, strategic decisions to follow the imperatives that marry impact and money and are grounded in the context in which the organization operates, and they must put financial resources into those areas that will generate impact and profitability.

The Unsustainable Organization

The Matrix Map will not always point to a sustainable future. Some organizations will find that they don't see a financially viable strategy going forward. For some, the Matrix Map confirms existing suspicions and fears. For others, discussion of the Matrix Map may be how the organization comes to understand that it has reached its end.

Usually by the time an organization gets to this point, there have already been efforts to move or add business lines. A new fundraising idea may have been tried, or new donors may have been approached. Entrance fees or ticket prices may have been raised. For whatever combination of reasons, the organization just may not be able to see a direction toward sustainability.

The Matrix Map will be an important piece of the decision about whether to approach another organization for a merger. It can also aid decisions about who can take over programs and which organizations may be good prospects. Look at the Heart programs to see whether one might become a Star in the setting of another organization, or look at a tiny Money Tree that might combine well with another organization's Money Tree. When you approach a potential merger partner, remember that your potential partner may not know your organization's current business lines well and may know only about one of your Stop Sign efforts. Quickly creating a Matrix Map for your potential partner's organization, and then another one for a combined organization, is a useful way to see what an integrated strategy might look like for a post-merger organization.

Sometimes organizations close not by quietly and tidily ceasing operations but by flaming out in a blaze of mission glory. When a youth skiing organization felt that it had only enough funds for another eighteen months, leaders chose to offer a longer program for the last ski season instead of using what had been the postseason period to try to raise money. For a dance troupe, the choice may be to throw everything into a better, high-impact final season and forget about sustainability after the season.

If this is your situation, remember that not many great restaurants last even twenty years. Doing something valuable for the years of your organization's existence was a meaningful contribution to the community.

The organization's impact was due in part to its ability to gather around it a community with shared values. As you close the organization, bring your community together to celebrate your achievements and affirm the values and goals that will now seek realization in other venues.

EVALUATING DECISIONS

For many organizations, once a decision has been made, there is seldom a moment to look back and evaluate how the decision process worked. Senior management and boards should occasionally evaluate how the decision-making process has worked, how it might have been improved or streamlined, and so forth. This is different from determining whether a decision has turned out right. For example, Midtown Multiservice Center seemed to have made a good decision by choosing to move its annual summer street festival to the fall so that local merchants could sell holiday gifts. But on the day of the festival, it rained. Regardless of how that decision turned out, the question is whether adequate information was used in the decision process. Did the decision makers even consider the greater likelihood of rain at that time of the year? No process and no type or amount of information can guarantee the right decision 100 percent of the time, but evaluation of the decision process allows you to make adjustments that increase your chances of success.

──────────────── **SUMMARY** ────────────────

Seeing your business model in the form of a Matrix Map can be a very empowering experience. Using the Matrix Map's strategic imperatives to make creative and strategic decisions allows your organization to be sustainable. There are numerous reasons why groups avoid decisions. But with a rigorous process, discipline, and leadership, a group can face challenges and meet them. Leaders should choose the criteria for success at the start and then engage in a generative process that allows the group to focus on alternatives and choose one on the basis of the selected criteria. Decision making is not an easy process, and there are many ways for groups to avoid making decisions. But true leaders do not use the available information to shrink from decisions. Instead, they guide the group in making decisions that are conscious and strategic, and then they continuously evaluate the organization's decision-making performance.

The Morphing Map

When a detective in a movie wants to analyze a crime scene, she usually looks at photographs. Likewise, when we want to analyze our organization, we look at the Matrix Map—a snapshot of our organization at any given time. But life resembles a movie more than a photograph, and just as life moves on from the motionless image in a photograph, the activities of an organization move on from their images in the Matrix Map.

In fact, the core activities of an organization actually move on their own over time, in a kind of migration or drift. A program that begins life as a Star may gradually evolve into a Stop Sign. Or it may evolve into a Heart and then become a Star again.

If you look at how your Matrix Map has changed over time, you can easily understand how your activities have moved. As a result, you can acknowledge those changes, anticipate further changes, and act on changes that have already occurred.

The constant migration of activities between and among the quadrants of the Matrix Map also points to the importance of adding new activities into the mix. As a Star gradually (or suddenly) loses its luster, it's important for new potential Stars to be incubating and growing.

In this chapter, we take a look at some of the classic migration paths that organizational activities follow, and we explain how to use the Matrix Map to understand and evaluate new opportunities or challenges, including the possibility of a merger.

chapter NINE

HOW STARS BECOME HEARTS

One of the more common migrations is from Star to Heart (see Figure 9.1). There are two common reasons for this migration—new competition and economic turmoil.

One irony of the nonprofit marketplace is that for-profits often step into growing fields and begin providing services to those who can afford them. Nonprofits that have balanced services to poor people with services to those who can afford them find themselves forced into more and more difficult markets.

For example, Midtown Multiservice Center originally offered a daycare program with affordable fees for families who needed childcare around the corner. When the program started, no other agencies were nearby, and Midtown established a fee-for-service model with a sliding scale.

But then an upscale childcare center came into town. This center is attached to a preschool offering a broad range of education along with daycare. As a result, the customer base of Midtown's daycare program changed. Those who were paying at the top of the sliding scale began to go to the new center. As a result, Midtown's program became unprofitable.

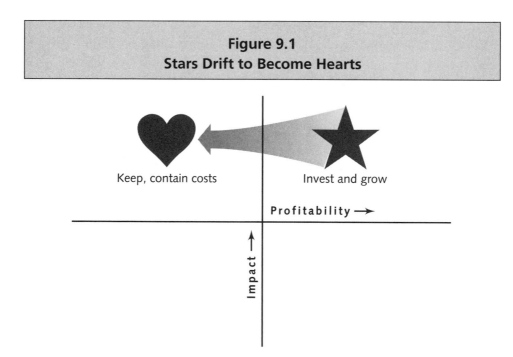

Figure 9.1
Stars Drift to Become Hearts

Keep, contain costs

Invest and grow

Profitability →

Impact ↑

Fortunately, the executive director saw the migration of the program from Star to Heart and knew that sustainability demanded that she change something. She looked around, analyzed the program, and determined why the migration had occurred. That analysis is part of what led to the organization's decision to open a Head Start program. This strategy allowed Midtown to offer more than just daycare and made the center eligible for government funds to serve its low-income clients. Now the program is a Star once again.

HEARTS ARE OFTEN THE PROGRAMS THAT STARTED THE ORGANIZATION

Sometimes programs can't change to play a deeper role for the organization, as Midtown's daycare program did. This is often the case for programs that have been offered by the organization from the beginning. For Everest Environmentalists, the vision of planting trees—creating an urban forest—was the inspiring idea and vision that got the organization off the ground. Planting trees (restoration and reforestation) was a physically attractive activity, brought neighbors together, and not only created street greenery but also signaled neighborhood improvement and neighbors' cooperation. The city government began to fund the organization's tree planting activities, and local community foundations also pitched in.

But the very success of the tree planting program brought commercial gardeners into the field. They underbid the nonprofit for tree planting because they bought cheaper trees and didn't spend time organizing neighborhoods for tree planting events. In a short period, tree planting went from being a Star program to losing its profitability because it was underbid for its government contract. In addition, the local foundations grew tired of funding the program and stopped after three years.

But the program was still dear to the staff, the volunteers, and the other donors, and no one could envision shutting it down or changing the core model on which it operated. The organization certainly could have planted trees more efficiently and more cost-effectively, but those modifications would not have brought the lasting change that can result from bringing a community together for planting. Besides, the community still wanted the program. It was the revenue strategy, not the program, that was broken.

The strategic imperative of the Heart still applies here—keep the program, but contain its costs. The important thing is to recognize the program's transition

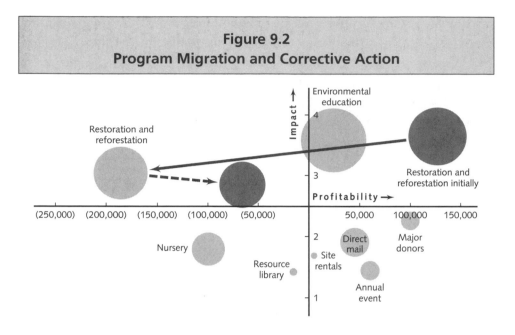

Figure 9.2
Program Migration and Corrective Action

from Star to Heart so that the organization can react and limit the program's financial subsidy to an affordable amount (see Figure 9.2). Everest could easily spend $450,000 every year on restoration and reforestation, but that would not be sustainable. Instead, the organization has chosen to keep this Heart but limit the financial loss to an affordable level while building up the organization's fundraising activities (Money Trees) and its Stars and thinking of additional revenue strategies for its Hearts.

DRIFTING FROM STAR TO HEART TO STOP SIGN

Figure 9.3 depicts the movement from Star to Heart to Stop Sign. Programs that become Stop Signs are often those that were vibrant and well funded in the past.

For example, Midtown Multiservice Center received a three-year grant several years ago to help permanent residents apply for U.S. citizenship. The program was welcomed by the community. It was immensely popular and well aligned with the community center's mission to serve the neighborhood, and the money allowed the center to hire two additional staff members. The citizenship program was a Star.

But the foundation that had made the grant moved away from immigration and citizenship as priority areas. It began to focus on microlending to low-income

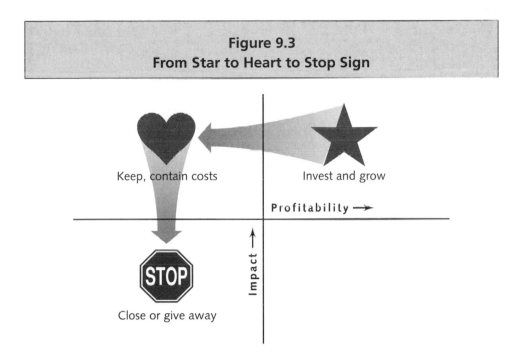

Figure 9.3
From Star to Heart to Stop Sign

Keep, contain costs

Invest and grow

Profitability →

Impact ↑

Close or give away

individuals starting their own businesses. For a while, small grants from other foundations were able to keep the program going. But the program was also attracting fewer participants—many permanent residents had now become citizens; the movement for citizenship was less visible, and those seeking citizenship had more complicated cases and situations than the first few waves of applicants.

The drop in funding alone might have moved the citizenship program from Star to Heart. But because of the decrease in interest, the program's impact also dropped dramatically. With fewer people interested in applying, and with those who did apply often needing legal help beyond what the center could provide, the organization had to face the reality that the citizenship program had moved from Star to Stop Sign (see Figure 9.4).

A Money Tree, too, can drift from Money Tree to Stop Sign. A fundraising activity can become stale over time and become less and less profitable. As a Money Tree becomes a Stop Sign, the organization must decide whether the activity can be reinvigorated or whether leaders must stop this activity and plant a new Money Tree.

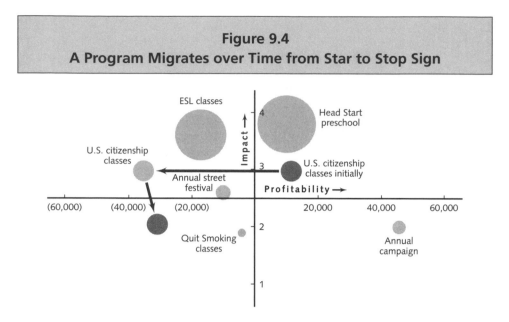

Figure 9.4
A Program Migrates over Time from Star to Stop Sign

CHANGING AN ACTIVITY FROM HEART OR STOP SIGN TO STAR

All of our scenarios so far have programs maturing and perhaps decreasing a bit in either impact or profitability. Don't activities ever migrate the other way? Yes, but programs don't drift on their own from being unprofitable to being profitable. In other words, Hearts don't become Stars through neglect. But Hearts are not always destined to be permanently unprofitable. If a program is valued and has a high enough impact to be a Heart, it's worth considering whether and how it could be made into a Star.

The most frequent way to turn a Heart into a Star is to put someone new in charge of it. For instance, despite the talents and contributions of Tempest Theater's current artistic director, it's possible that a new artistic director—perhaps someone more innovative, and with a national reputation—will bring a new vision that excites funders as well as audiences. And at Midtown Multiservice Center, the new after-school program director, who grew up working in his family's restaurant just a block away, sees a way to make the street festival the culmination of the youth program's activities. In this way, the street festival will not only increase its impact but also break even, thanks to the increased sponsorship of merchants and donors.

It's probably too risky to fire a program director who is competent but not stellar, in hopes of hiring a dynamic new leader. But if a program director is underperforming or leaves on his or her own, it's a time to consider whether the right new hire can turn a program around.

Another way to move from Heart to Star is to really consider both the value and the impact that a program has, along with the revenue strategy. In the for-profit sector, the term *value proposition* is used in discussions of why you would want to buy a product from a particular company. Why would you want to pay $3 for a cup of coffee from Starbucks? Similarly, we need to understand our Hearts better, realize why their impact is so high, and then communicate their impact value through our revenue strategy.

Recall the example of Everest Environmentalists, which was facing increasing competition from for-profit nurseries that were planting local street trees. The model that the nurseries used allowed more trees to be planted for the same amount of money. No wonder they received the government contract! But why was their model cheaper? Because, rather than taking the time to engage the community and volunteers, the nurseries simply hired people whose job it was to put the trees in the ground. As mentioned earlier, the Everest staff and volunteers couldn't envision changing their model. When they reflected on the overall framework, however, they thought of a new way of defining their impact. By bringing the community together, they had built in a long-term maintenance plan for the trees. Someone had to water the trees after they were planted. The for-profit nurseries relied on Mother Nature for rain, but the trees planted by Everest Environmentalists were watered by the very same volunteers who had planted them. As a result, more of the Everest-planted trees survived over time, having greater impact and ultimately providing greater value to the city.

It's difficult to recover funding and move a program from Heart to Star by thinking about impact. Nevertheless, it is important to make sure that you understand a program's true impact and can clearly articulate it.

WHEN THINGS DON'T MOVE AS EXPECTED

Sometimes even the best of intentions don't pan out as planned. An organization creates its Matrix Map, analyzes the strategic imperatives, and makes the hard decision to shut down a Stop Sign. As a result, however, the organization is even worse off financially. How did this happen?

As explained earlier, administrative expenses are allocated to program costs when the profitability of programs is determined. Even though administrative expenses aren't directly incurred by any one program, they are incurred in support of that program. Therefore, from the perspective of revenue strategy, the program should be able to cover its share of administrative costs. But what happens if it doesn't?

If you decide to close down or divest the program, you don't typically reduce your administrative expenses. They simply shift to the remaining programs. Some organizations go through the process of splitting out their administrative expenses and assessing their impact. But what truly is the impact of administration? This is a hard question to answer because administration by its very nature is something we need in order to function as a nonprofit organization. Figure 9.5 shows a nonprofit organization's administrative expenses allocated out to programs, and Figure 9.6 shows administrative expenses as an independent activity. Separating administrative expenses out has a significant impact on the organization's largest program, shelter services, since the majority of administrative costs have been allocated to that program. There may be reasons why the shelter services program does not cover its entire share of administrative expenses. For example, limits on overhead may have been imposed by government contracts

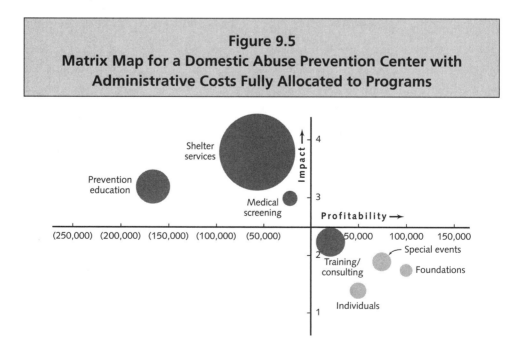

Figure 9.5
Matrix Map for a Domestic Abuse Prevention Center with Administrative Costs Fully Allocated to Programs

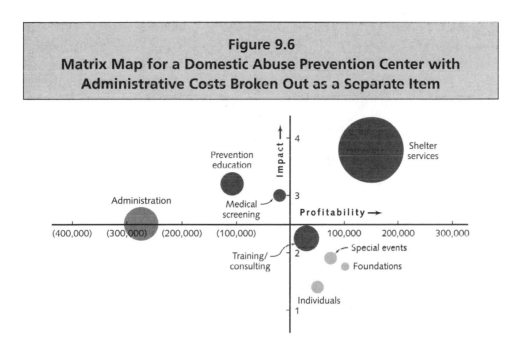

Figure 9.6
Matrix Map for a Domestic Abuse Prevention Center with Administrative Costs Broken Out as a Separate Item

and foundations. Factors like this one are important to consider when it comes to devising strategies for additional revenue.

When making decisions, we must think through not the impact but rather the efficiency of our administration. Not many nonprofits have bloated accounting departments, but many do have technology that is two, three, or even four generations old. What is the impact on efficiency of using such dated technology? What would happen if you invested some money in technology? Could you improve efficiency? Also, as an organization increases or decreases in size, leaders need to consider the effects on administration, in particular the finance and technology departments. Although administrative costs don't go away when a department is shut down, it is also true that a $1 million organization does not usually need as many accountants as a $3.5 million organization. When we look at our Matrix Map to understand strategic imperatives and make decisions, we must remember that a portion of each program's expenses are administrative.

ANALYZING NEW OPPORTUNITIES

Just as your Matrix Map may change over time as your programs change, it can also be used to analyze new programs or opportunities. If senior managers understand

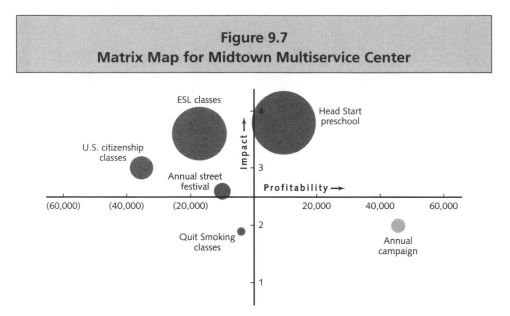

Figure 9.7
Matrix Map for Midtown Multiservice Center

the current business model and the organization's route to sustainability, they can make decisions about what the goals of various programs need to be. For example, recall Midtown Multiservice Center's Matrix Map (see Figure 9.7). As Midtown's leaders were discussing their strategic imperatives and making decisions, a foundation approached with a proposal for the center to add a fitness program. The center had long been cultivating this foundation, and the leaders were very excited to suddenly be having this conversation. On its own, the idea of starting a new community fitness program seemed like a good idea. But as the leaders looked at the interrelationships of all the organization's activities on the Matrix Map, it became clear that the center could not afford another Heart.

The center had a couple of options. These included passing on the opportunity because it wouldn't have as high an impact as the current activities, asking the foundation to fund the new fitness program in its entirety so that it would break even, or cutting back on another program and subsidizing the fitness program internally. If it had been determined that a fitness program would have a higher impact than other programs, then it would have been appropriate to reduce those programs in the interest of subsidizing the cost of the new fitness program. Again, leadership and decision making are necessary, but the Matrix Map provides information about the context in which decisions are made.

USING THE MATRIX MAP TO ANALYZE
A POSSIBLE MERGER

The issue of mergers creates another opportunity to use the Matrix Map as an exploratory tool. Given the current economic downturn, there has been a rising chorus, primarily of funders, calling for mergers among nonprofit organizations. The conventional wisdom often expressed in these arguments is that there are too many small nonprofits, and that combining the efforts of these organizations will increase the sustainability and efficiency of the nonprofit sector. A rebound in the economy may lessen such calls, but with the nonprofit sector growing at a substantial rate and funders feeling overwhelmed by requests, we can expect this topic to remain open for years to come.

The decision about whether to merge is multifaceted and involves not only finances and program similarity but also organizational culture and governance. Just as we use the Matrix Map to evaluate new opportunities and understand the effect that pursuing an opportunity will have on impact and profitability, we can also use the Matrix Map as a tool to better understand what a merged organization would look like and how it would function.

As discussions of a possible merger begin, it is helpful if both organizations have a solid understanding of themselves. Creating a Matrix Map is a good way to give a visual demonstration of the activities in which the organization engages and how they interrelate. For example, two organizations are considering a merger. The first, Organization A, is a shelter for runaway youth that also offers programs in mental health counseling and school and career coaching. In addition to these activities, Organization A has a major donor activity and an annual event. Organization A's matrix map, shown in Figure 9.8, demonstrates that the organization's programs have a substantial amount of impact, but that together they barely sustain Organization A, even with the efforts of major donors and an annual event subsidizing the core programs.

Organization A is considering a merger with Organization B, a mental health agency that provides counseling and therapy to all age groups. Organization B's core activities are group therapy and one-on-one counseling as well as an outreach campaign that aims to educate the public about mental illness. Organization B's programs are funded primarily by government contracts, with an annual fund-raising event to make up the difference. Its Matrix Map is shown in Figure 9.9.

From an operational standpoint, the two organizations shared complementary programs, and both would have benefited from a stronger financial base.

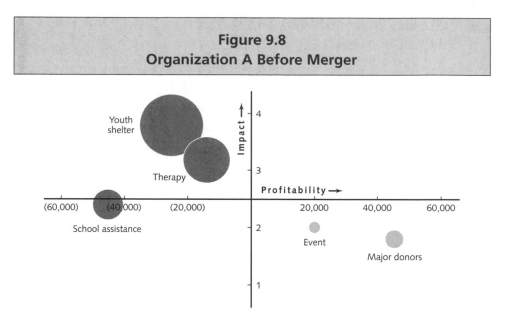

Figure 9.8
Organization A Before Merger

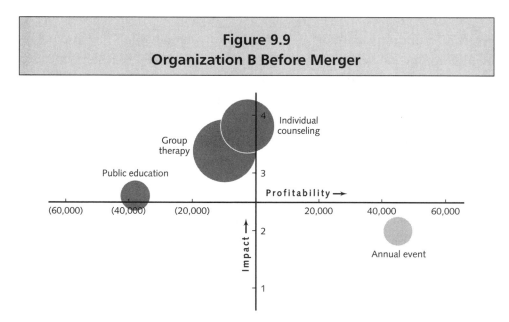

Figure 9.9
Organization B Before Merger

As they considered merging, they found preparing a Matrix Map a useful way to facilitate discussion of what the merged organization might look like. Here are some of the questions that arose:

- *Which core activities would be combined, and how?* Organization A had a therapy program that was very similar to the individual counseling program of Organization B. The boards envisioned that these two activities would be combined, and so when they prepared a merged Matrix Map, they reconstructed the finances and raised the potential impact for this combination. In addition to these programs, the boards also looked at the fundraising activities. Both organizations held annual events, which the boards felt would be combined into only one event. The committees examined the donor lists to arrive at new financial projections based on the combined events.

- *Would any revenues be lost?* Oftentimes when similar organizations merge, there is overlap among donors of all types—foundations, individuals, and government agencies. It is easy to think that gifts from these overlapped sources might be combined in a merged organization, but donors rarely maintain their exact gift patterns. For example, if a donor used to give $100 to Organization A and $50 to Organization B, it is unlikely that the merged organization will now receive $150 from this donor. Therefore, as leaders explore the profitability of a merged organization's activities, they need to consider what the dropoff may be when donor lists overlap.

- *Will there be efficiency savings?* Just as they look at overlap among donors, organizations discussing a merger must consider what it truly would require to operate a merged organization and see if there are any savings based on likely efficiencies. There are potential savings in the accounting department, although this is an opportunity to really dig into underlying assumptions and ask what it will take to support a bigger, merged organization.

Although these questions should be answered during any merger-exploration process, regardless of whether the Matrix Map is used, the Matrix Map does help to structure the conversation as organizations begin to create something new. A merged organization formed from Organizations A and B might look like the one shown in Figure 9.10. Using this map, the two organizations can better understand the strategic imperatives of their core activities and can more proactively create a merged organization that is programmatically and financially more sustainable.

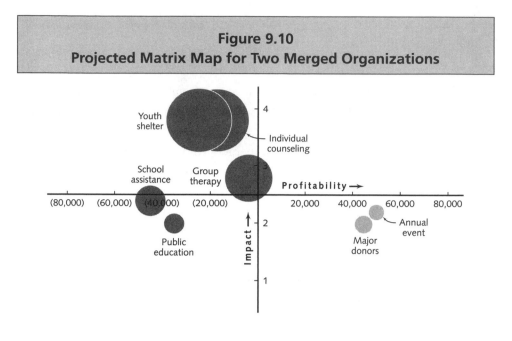

Figure 9.10
Projected Matrix Map for Two Merged Organizations

SUMMARY

The one constant in the world today is change. Whether because of the changing needs of constituents or the finicky tastes of funders, programs that were wildly successful ten years ago can struggle today to remain relevant. The Matrix Map shows this change over time, with programs morphing from Stars to Hearts and sometimes to Stop Signs—and, we hope, back again. The Matrix Map provides a picture of our business model at any given time, and through the imperatives we follow as well as the decisions we make, we aim to reconfigure that picture. By choosing our trajectory and then monitoring the Matrix Map over time, we can see if our organization is heading toward or away from a sustainable position. We can also use the Matrix Map to evaluate unexpected challenges or pleasant opportunities and understand their implications for our business model. When an organization uses the Matrix Map to present its business model in a visually engaging manner that board and staff members can understand, regardless of their knowledge of the financial aspects of the organization, leaders can engage in a robust discussion and prepare themselves to make continuous strategic decisions with an orientation toward sustainability.

PART FOUR

The Business Logic of Nonprofit Income Types

One common reaction to the experience of looking at the Matrix Map is to conclude that the organization simply needs to raise more money. But we know from experience that there is little that is simple about generating new income, either through traditional philanthropic contributions or through earned-revenue strategies.

One reason for this reaction is the possibility that not everyone understands what it typically takes to be successful with a given revenue strategy. For example, board members may see another, similar organization enjoying great success with individual contributions, but they may not understand the significance of that organization's having connected with thousands of individuals during its thirty-five-year history.

In Part Four, we deepen our discussion of revenue strategies by examining some aspects of the more common revenue types, focusing on contributed philanthropic income (Chapter Ten) and earned income (Chapter Eleven).

A Look at the Business Logic of Types of Donations

This book works with business lines as building blocks. Gala dinners, direct mail, government contracts, and fee-for-service arrangements are analyzed for their financial impact and their mission impact. But so far we have not fully explained these business lines. Perhaps more important, we have not discussed how you should consider them or how you can get started using them if your organization has them under consideration.

This chapter and Chapter Eleven examine the business logic underneath a few of these common business lines. Although managers and board members are often familiar with who funds what in the organization, an understanding of the business logic is useful when it comes to making decisions about how an activity fits into the overall business model of the organization. In particular, board members often have less experience with and understanding of what makes nonprofit income strategies tick, which makes it harder for board members to assess in advance whether a particular activity should be added to the organizational portfolio.

The business lines chosen for this chapter do not comprise a complete universe. They are a selection of those that are available and appropriate to community nonprofits, and that are commonly considered by them. Therefore, this summary is not a detailed how-to guide, nor is it a plan for determining an activity's feasibility. It is a fast primer that amplifies the ideas discussed elsewhere in this book, and it may awaken new ideas or insights for board members.

In this chapter, we discuss contributed income, or donations. For each income stream you'll find a definition as well as a basic description of how it works, tips on what it takes to be successful with it, the organizational contexts where it often works best, and suggestions for getting started.

INTERNET FUNDRAISING

Because Internet fundraising is relatively new, we'll start here with a fast recap of Internet fundraising types and how they work, and then we'll go on to discuss where various vehicles are best suited.

Here are the key types of Internet fundraising, with descriptions of how they work:

• *Using your Web site to accept donations and sell goods and services (such as books or workshops).* It's not hard to add a "Donate Now" button to your Web site that is managed by one of the dozens of nonprofit or commercial services, such as Groundspring or Network for Good, which take a percentage of donations made. It's easy to set up, but it's like a mailbox—people don't start sending in checks just because you have one.

• *Sending an e-mail newsletter to constituents and including requests for donations.* Because e-mail goes to the inbox of the member or constituent, a newsletter is an effective way to create your own newspaper. A "Donate Now" button makes it easy for people to click through to donate, but some recipients will want something they can print and mail in with a check.

• *Selling advertisements on your Web site.* If you have a large number of visitors to your site, you can seek nonprofit and for-profit advertisers who would be interested in placing ads on your site. Many organizations find that advertising doesn't pay in the trade-off between revenue, on the one hand, and, on the other, the time spent seeking advertising, not to mention possible negative reactions to advertising.

• *"Renting" space on your Web site to commercial companies, such as Google or Amazon, and thus getting a commission on items sold by them through your site.* Amazon, for example, uses an automated scan to identify the topics discussed on your Web site and then chooses books on the same subjects to advertise on your site. For some organizations, this is a useful service as well as an easy but low-revenue project. But you should be careful—one international exchange site found that Google's placements were frequently about overseas mail-order brides.

• *Holding an online auction.* Both silent auctions and live auctions are traditional moneymakers for many nonprofits. In the Internet version of an auction, a nonprofit contracts with an online provider, such as BiddingForGood or eBay, which takes a portion of the purchase prices. Nonprofit staff and volunteers obtain donated items, although it's also possible to contract for items on "consignment" through these services—adding a much larger inventory, but taking away some of the personal feeling that community nonprofit auctions often have. The nonprofit sends e-mails over the auction period (perhaps two months), asking people to bid. An online auction can be successful for an organization that has strong volunteer management of the auction, obtains a sizable number of donations, and has a large e-mail list. An online auction is particularly worthwhile if you are auctioning specialty products (such as ethnic jewelry or products for people with low hearing) that your audience may have trouble finding elsewhere.

• *Fundraising on Facebook and other social media (Twitter, Delicious, and so on).* Social media are better suited to individuals reaching individuals than to organizations reaching individuals, with the exception of well-known organizations such as the Red Cross. As a result, most organizations typically do best when individual staff members and volunteers write in their own voices to their own networks and ask for funding, in the same way that individuals seek pledges for walkathons. A volunteer-based Facebook campaign typically raises only $500 to $5,000, but it also keeps members involved. At least for now, nonprofits are having more success using social media to build connections and presence than using them to raise money.

In general, Internet fundraising does better for organizations that integrate an e-mail newsletter approach with a friendly Web site. If you don't already have the basic requirements, you may not want to invest in them solely on the basis of fundraising prospects. The key necessary components for successful Internet fundraising include these:

• A sizable constituency or audience, especially one that is already engaged through the Internet in other kinds of activities (the constituency can be consumers and beneficiaries, such as patrons of a dance company or families of children with cancer, or it can include supporters of your cause, such as volunteers and people who believe in your work)

- An organizational Web site with clear goals for its audience and a clear vision of what it intends to achieve, and how it intends to do so

- An e-mail newsletter or a plan for sending regular e-mails to people on the list(s)

- E-mail addresses and other Internet-connection information from all constituents through all other activities (such as events, workshops, volunteer days, and so forth)

- Capable and reliable technical support

- A vision for the Internet strategy that is championed by at least one person on the management team

- For the organization that wants to raise funds through social media, at least one person (a staff member or a volunteer) who will consistently and creatively establish a presence for himself or herself and for the organization and communicate the organization's values, work, and opportunities (this will be as much about the individual as about the organization, so make sure you choose someone who understands this and is in tune with the organization's style)

To get started, choose one person or a small committee to explore the Internet fundraising that is being conducted by organizations similar to yours. It's best to start small and then grow rather than invest significant time and money in an area that is new to your organization. Because there is so much hype around Internet fundraising, it's easy to feel pressured at the outset to launch overambitious projects. Proceed with caution.

MAJOR GIFTS

Nonprofits use the term *major gifts* as a shorthand way of talking about substantial financial donations from individuals. We've used a "frequently asked questions" (FAQ) format in this section to address how a major gifts program works, where it works best, and how to get started with one.

What dollar amount makes a donation a major gift? The level at which a gift is considered major varies greatly from one organization to another. In some organizations a major gift is $100, and in others major gifts start at $10,000. If your organization does not already have a well-developed program for obtaining major gifts, set a threshold where you can expect to get five gifts at or above that level within the first year.

Who is asked for major gifts? Who does the asking? Major gifts programs usually involve volunteers (such as board members) asking for donations from two types of people—individuals whom they know personally, and prospective donors who have been contacted initially by staff members. And because the size of a major gift is usually such that the donor can't make a fast, impulsive decision, most major gifts are solicited through in-person meetings.

What's the business logic behind major gifts? A core fundraising principle is to move donors up the gift ladder and have them make larger and larger donations over time. This usually involves asking the donor through a different vehicle, asking in a different way, or asking for something different:

- First donation: $35 by check, in response to a mail appeal
- Second donation: $50 renewal gift in response to a phone call from a volunteer
- Third donation: $175 to attend a special event at a level that includes some perks in addition to the ticket
- Fourth donation (a year later): $500 in response to a phone call from someone the donor knows
- Fifth donation: A multiyear pledge of $500 per year for five years
- Sixth donation: Purchase of a table at a special event at the sponsor level for $1,800
- Subsequent donation (two years later): $10,000 for a special project (such as a new playground or a special advocacy campaign)
- Final donation (many years later): $300,000, left to the organization in the donor's will

Aside from the dollars raised, what are the advantages of a major gifts program?

- The gifts are typically unrestricted.
- The program uses contacts beyond those of the staff.

- When the program works, major gifts are cost-effective, with a high return on investment.
- The process of identifying and involving donors builds the organization's constituency.
- Individuals often make major gifts several years in a row.

What's not so great about major gifts?

- It takes years to build substantial and reliable revenue from a major gifts program, and sometimes that never happens.
- Volunteers may be reluctant to ask people they know for donations.
- Staff and volunteers may have few relationships with people of enough means to make major gifts.
- Donors often get tired of giving after a few years.

Which organizations do best with major gifts? Major gifts programs are best for organizations with the following resources and attributes:

- A constituency, especially one that goes beyond direct beneficiaries
- Board members and senior staff who are culturally competent with respect to the people who will be asked for donations (not everyone can establish rapport with wealthy individuals)
- The funds to invest in a multiyear effort to start a major gifts program
- A strong enough organizational ethos to resist being excessively influenced by major donors or resenting people who are wealthy enough to make major gifts

What's needed to get started with major gifts?

- Two or three board members who champion the idea and lead the effort among board members to identify and ask people for major gifts
- Board members and other volunteers who know people with significant financial means and are willing to ask them for donations
- Capable staff support, including involvement on the part of the executive director
- Perfectly reliable systems for making sure that donations are tracked, donors are thanked, and renewals are requested appropriately

ANNUAL APPEALS AND MEMBERSHIP RENEWAL CAMPAIGNS

Fundraising consultants will often remind you that more than 75 percent of donations (as distinct from total income) come from individuals (rather than from institutions, such as foundations and corporations), and that the primary reason why people give to a nonprofit is that someone asks.

Despite the term *annual appeal*, there is not only a single time each year when the organization asks individuals to make contributions. The annual appeal usually goes out at the same time every year (such as in November), and it usually goes out to all the organization's contacts (not just to those whose only interest, for example, is supporting the organization's summer camp).

Most annual appeals combine a few techniques. The typical appeal consists of the following elements:

- A letter to organizational contacts
- Follow-up telephone calls
- An e-mail message to the organization's e-mail list

The Business Logic of Annual Appeals

Donors, members, and constituents are familiar with being asked for donations on an annual basis. Making an annual donation is an easy way for them to support your work, to feel connected to your organization, to honor someone who is connected with your organization, to be recognized in your annual report, and so forth. Because annual appeals don't need to cost much, and because they're speaking to what is called a "warm" list, they typically net substantially more than the financial investment. For example, a first-class letter with a report to the community is mailed to eight hundred contacts and friends of the organization. The cost, apart from staff time used for writing the letter and stuffing envelopes, is $900 plus the cost of a follow-up thank-you, and the letter elicits seventy-five responses and a total of $3,000. In addition, although an annual appeal is not typically a key part of a major gifts program, it does identify people interested in your organization who can be contacted as possible major donors.

Who Should Be Asked in the Annual Appeal

Quite simply, the organization should ask anyone for whom it has contact information and who might have an interest in the organization's mission:

- *Recent donors.* A person who has made a donation within the last twelve months is usually called a *current donor.* Even someone who made a donation just a couple of months ago should be asked in the annual appeal to give again. For such donors, the annual appeal letter will serve as an overall update about the organization, and many of these donors may choose to give again.

- *Alumni of the organization.* This group includes former staff members and former board members.

- *Clients, patrons, season ticket holders, and anyone who has benefited from the organization's programs or who has seen firsthand the power of its work.*

- *Volunteers.* People in this group can be thanked in the annual appeal and asked to make a donation as well. Volunteers have seen the impact of the organization, and hopefully they also appreciate the community surrounding the organization.

- *Significant vendors to the organization.* This group may include the organization's attorney, its auditor, its printer, its insurance broker, its strategic planning consultant, and others.

- *Leaders or members of advisory committees.*

When People Should Be Asked

The most common time for organizations to ask for donations is toward the end of the year, in December, when people are in the giving spirit and usually make their charitable contributions. You don't need to hold to this rule if there is another time of year that might make sense for your organization's mission (for example, Japanese organizations tend to ask in February, around the Day of Remembrance, which commemorates the internment of Japanese Americans during World War II). An environmental organization might use Earth Day as an opportunity to make its annual appeal, and a breast cancer organization might make its appeal around Mother's Day. Think of your mission and the calendar, and see if there is a time that makes more sense for your appeal than the end of the year. If you ask earlier in the year, you can always follow up with those who didn't respond at the end of the year, to see if they might be willing to donate then.

How People Should Be Asked

There are many ways you can go about making your appeal, but what you do will depend on the format in which you have the contact information for the donor. Year-end letters are a fairly common way of making an annual appeal, but you need potential donors' names and street addresses. Likewise, if you only have e-mail addresses, an e-mail appeal would be the right way to go, perhaps combined with an appeal on your Web site and with the ability to give online.

How Much to Ask For

If possible, it's a good idea to remind each current donor of his or her last gift and ask for another donation at the same or a higher level. There may also be a special project for which you can request a donation significantly higher than the last gift.

What It Takes to Succeed with an Annual Appeal

First, you need names, names, and more names. The success of an annual appeal depends primarily on how many people you have to ask. There is no exact number of people you should have on your list of people to ask, but certainly the more you have, the merrier you will be. Collecting names and addresses takes some forethought. Do you interact with people who have the ability to give? Do you have a way to collect their names and addresses or connect with them on Facebook or on some other social networking site? Sitting down in November to think about whom to ask is usually sitting down too late. Your organization may ask only once a year, but you should think all year about whom to ask and how you will contact those potential donors when the time comes.

Second, you need time for the annual appeal. It takes time to write a letter or an e-mail and get it right, and it takes time to distribute it. Don't underestimate how much time this will be. And if the appeal goes well, it will also take time to process all the thank-you letters!

Organizations That Typically Do Well with an Annual Appeal

There are two types of organizations in which an annual appeal usually works best: the organization with constituents (often members) who use the organization's services or understand the benefit that the organization provides to the community and who have the ability to make a contribution, and the organization that has a well-connected, engaged board willing to ask friends and contacts for donations.

Constituents who use the organization's services or care passionately about the organization are most likely to respond to a request for a donation. The organization to which they donate can be of any type, from a childcare center to an environmental organization to an art museum. These people already understand and value the organization, and it's often easier to ask them for donations than to introduce the organization to someone new.

Getting Started

To get started with an annual appeal, ask yourself if you have enough people from whom to seek donations. And do you have a way of reaching your potential donors? These are the first two questions to ask when you're getting started. The biggest challenge of the annual appeal is figuring out how best to reach out to potential donors. Think first about how to obtain the names and addresses (e-mail or otherwise) of your potential donors, and then concern yourself with your message and with delivering it in a way that will elicit donations.

DIRECT MAIL TO A WARM LIST

The term *direct mail* refers to requests made to individuals for donations, typically through letters. Large-scale direct mail programs involve renting lists with tens of thousands of names, mailing millions of letters each year, and bringing in hundreds of thousands of dollars.

Here, we discuss only direct mail programs that involve constituents such as prior donors, volunteers, former staff and board members, ticket buyers, and friends of board members. This is called using a "warm" list (a "hot" list is composed of people who have made recent donations to the organization, and a cold list is a rented or borrowed list).

The Business Logic of Direct Mail to a Warm List

Because the letters are sent to contacts of the organization, a relatively good percentage can be expected to result in donations. (Sending to a cold list typically results in less than 1 percent of the mailed pieces bringing in donations, but second and third mailings to a cold list will often result in additional gifts.)

First-time gifts from individuals are usually modest—say, $10 to $150. If a donor is appropriately thanked and involved, however, it may be possible to move him or her up the gift ladder. Direct mail to a warm list is used partly to raise money and partly to identify people who can be asked (by phone or in person) for larger gifts.

The Downside of a Direct Mail Appeal

Board and staff members may be reluctant to send personal notes to people who are otherwise not connected with the organization. In addition, the complex logistics of direct mail (decisions about the envelope, about the letter itself, about whether to enclose an action card, about whether to use a stamp or metered postage, and so forth) create a kind of bog in which it is easy to become mired. Finally, writing a compelling letter and making sure that recipients open the envelope may be new skills for those put in charge of a direct mail campaign.

Involvement of Board Members

Each board member typically submits a list of names and addresses (say, twenty-five contacts from each member) of people to whom donation requests will be mailed. Board members often write a personal note on each letter, and they even write their names on the outside of the envelope (to get it opened).

As donations come in, it is important to let board members know that their contacts have given so that board members can give them personal expressions of thanks in addition to the staff-generated thank-you.

Direct Mail Requests via E-mail

A direct mail request can be sent by e-mail, but not usually with the same text used for a letter. A request by e-mail must be a highly personalized, authentic message from the sender. Many board members and volunteers are much more reluctant to send out such messages than they are to write notes on a printed letter for mass distribution.

Organizations That Typically Do Well with Direct Mail to a Warm List

Organizations that do well with this approach have the following resources and attributes:

- Up-to-date lists of constituents
- Board members, senior staff members, and volunteers who will send the mail pieces, with personal notes, to their own contact lists

- Access to strong writing skills
- The ability and willingness to follow up with donors and move them to additional gifts at higher levels

Getting Started

Here is what an organization needs to get started with this kind of direct mail appeal:

- A warm list or lists
- A writer, preferably one who has experience asking for donations by mail
- Board members' agreement to write personal notes on the appeal letters and send the letters to their own contact lists
- A timetable, and someone who relentlessly keeps everyone accountable to it

FOUNDATION GRANTS

Foundation grants consist of monies received from foundations, typically through some sort of granting process. Foundation fundraising is a staple of many nonprofits for the following reasons:

- *Foundations are visible, and you can get access.* Foundations, unlike individual donors, are known and readily visible in our communities. You can ask anyone in the nonprofit community who the local foundations are, and you will likely hear the names of two or three. Foundations are also listed in the local foundation directory and may have Web sites that lay out their guidelines and processes for giving grants.

- *Foundations have to give away money.* Foundations are required by the IRS to give 5 percent or more of their assets each year (with some averaging). Because the amount varies with the value of their assets, foundations often give much less when reversals in the stock market cause their stock portfolios to lose value.

- *Foundations tend to make substantial gifts.* Whereas individuals may give $25 to $50, foundations tend to give away anywhere from $1,500 to $100,000 or more. Organizations that are starting out often turn to foundations because of a perceived higher return on their investment of the time they spend to solicit the donation. We say "perceived" because if you add up the time spent, the return on this investment may not actually be higher than what might have been obtained with other strategies.

- *Foundations sometimes give multiyear grants.* Although this is increasingly rare, some foundations still do make multiyear gifts to nonprofit organizations, letting them concentrate on carrying out their programs instead of on more fundraising.

Basic Types of Foundations and How to Find Out About Them

Not all foundations make grants to nonprofits. Some use their monies to operate their own programs. Others contract for services with for-profit businesses. The following are the most common types of grantmaking foundations:

- *Private family foundations.* Most foundations are private foundations, typically started by a family with personal wealth (the donors receive a tax deduction for the money they put into the foundation). If the founding donor is still alive, he or she may behave more like an individual donor than like an institution, where grantmaking is managed by staff members. Most private foundations are small; according to the Foundation Center, half of family foundations give out less than $50,000 per year (see the Foundation Center, *Key Facts on Family Foundations,* 2007). And then there's the Bill and Melinda Gates Foundation!

- *Community foundations.* A community foundation is one that aggregates the gifts of many donors. Usually community foundations are organized by geographical area (for example, the Memphis Community Foundation), but sometimes they are organized around interest groups (for example, a women's foundation, a Latino foundation, or a gay/lesbian foundation).

- *Donor-advised funds.* In a donor-advised fund, a commercial firm (such as Fidelity or Schwab) and community foundations hold pools of money that are given out at the direction of the donor. For instance, a donor might place $50,000 in a donor-advised fund (thereby getting a tax deduction in the year of the donation) and then stipulate that the money be given out to nonprofits over the next five years. Reaching a donor-advised fund automatically means reaching the donor (see "Major Gifts," earlier in this chapter).

- *Corporate foundations.* These foundations are discussed in the next section, "Corporate Foundations and Corporate Giving Programs."

- *Trusts controlled by banks, law firms, and so forth.* In some cases, a trust is created out of a will. This is an arrangement whereby a bank, a law firm, or a designated person or group gives away funds annually after the donor has died. In many cases, a committee of perhaps five or ten individuals chooses the trust's grantees each year. In seeking money from one of these trusts, it is best to know who in your constituency may be on such a committee.

A first step in finding foundations is to visit the Foundation Center, either at one of its locations (which you can visit for free) or by going to the organization's Web site (www.foundationcenter.org, which operates on the basis of paid subscriptions). On the Web site, you can search by funding area or by geographical area. But many foundations are not listed there, and so it is just as important to ask local foundations and nonprofits for suggestions.

Organizations That Typically Do Well with Foundation Funding

Foundation funding works best for organizations that have the following resources and attributes:

- Location in a geographical region with many foundations—typically an urban area with a history of wealth (most foundations give in their local areas)

- Access to strong writing skills

- A cause that is popular with foundations (although there is enormous variety in foundations' interests, most foundations shy away from controversial causes; it's easier to find foundation funding for education than for prison reform)

The Downside of Foundation Funding

- Foundations often take several weeks or even months between receiving a proposal and issuing a check, or even a rejection letter.

- Most foundation grants are restricted to particular programs or activities. As a result, they may not cover the full costs of the funded work. The organization will need to raise other funds to make the project financially neutral.

- Foundations may ask for more information than you can easily produce or feel comfortable sharing.

- Some foundations will want to take an active role in the management and direction of your organization. They see this as helpful advising and coaching, but you may or may not see it that way.

- Some foundations implicitly require quite a bit of time from grantees, asking them to attend convenings, meet with foundation staff, meet with people suggested by the program officer, and so forth.

CORPORATE FOUNDATIONS AND CORPORATE GIVING PROGRAMS

Corporate gifts are gifts from businesses and corporations. Gifts can come either directly from a corporation itself or from a foundation that a large corporation has established to handle its philanthropic giving.

The Business Logic of Corporate Gifts

From the corporation's point of view, the business logic of corporate gifts is associated with its business strategy. In addition to supporting the community, a corporation may want to publicize the company within a key customer demographic, or to meet regulatory guidelines for community investment, or to provide employees with team-building volunteer activities. As one banking executive commented in a speech, "The purpose of our corporate foundation is to increase shareholder value."

From a nonprofit point of view, the business logic of corporate gifts is that such gifts are often unrestricted, and although they're relatively small (typically $500 to $5,000), they may not require a large investment of time. Working with a local corporation can provide a nonprofit with grants and noncash contributions (such as furniture), and the corporation's employees receive opportunities to serve as volunteers.

Organizations That Typically Do Well with Corporate Gifts

Organizations that do well with corporate foundations and corporate giving programs have the following resources and attributes:

- Location in the headquarter city of a corporation and, to a much lesser degree, in a community where the corporation has a plant, a large retail operation, or another large facility with many employees

- Board members and volunteers who are corporate employees, preferably at the top (some corporations match the donations of their employees, and others give preference to organizations with which their employees are involved)

- A noncontroversial cause and/or a cause related to the work of the corporation (for example, Kraft Foods funds mostly in the area of nutrition)

Getting Started

To get started, make a list of the corporations in your local area that are aligned in some way with your organization's mission. Then circulate the list among your board of directors and see if anyone on the board has contacts in those corporations.

PLANNED GIVING

Most donations are made by individuals who give cash, and who receive a tax deduction at the end of the year. In contrast, planned giving refers to donations (of cash, stock, real estate, and so on) that are structured for tax purposes so that the donor receives the tax deduction in his lifetime but the organization receives the funds after his death.

Leaving Money in a Will Versus Planned Giving

Leaving an organization money in one's will—a bequest—is a simple type of planned giving whereby both the donation and the tax deduction take place at the time of the donor's death. A bequest can be as simple as "I leave $10,000 to Tempest Theater" or "I leave 1 percent of my after-tax estate to the Midtown Multiservice Center."

The term *planned giving* generally refers more specifically to a set of gift types based on provisions in United States tax law. As an illustration, a charitable remainder trust (CRT) can be established by a donor who is confident about his financial future. He donates an asset (say, an apartment building) to a nonprofit. He receives a tax deduction for the value of the building, and the rental income from the building continues to go to the donor for as long as he lives. The nonprofit neither receives any income nor assumes control of the building until after the donor's death. It's more complicated than this, and there are many variations, but that's the idea.

Other types of assets donated in this way are life insurance policies, IRAs, stocks and securities, cash, and personal property, such as artworks. If the asset does not generate income (for example, a painting in the donor's living room), the donor keeps the asset until his death and receives the tax deduction in the year he makes the donation. The nonprofit receives the painting after the donor's death, at which time the organization is free to sell it or otherwise use it.

Organizations That Typically Do Well with Planned Giving

Organizations that do well with planned giving have the following resources and attributes:

- Older donors, and constituents with strong loyalty to the organization
- Longevity (a donor may be making her will but expects to live another twenty years, so she'll want to give to an organization she feels confident will still be around in twenty years, such as the Sierra Club, the ACLU, or the NAACP)

Getting Started

Is there an easy way to get started with planned giving? Yes.

Ask your board members to consider putting the organization in their wills. If someone does so, be sure to let the other board members know.

In your newsletter or other communications with clients, patrons, members, patients, former staff, and others, suggest that your organization be named in their wills, and let them know that if they would like to talk with you about planned giving, such as a CRT, you will be glad to work with them and their attorneys. (And as soon as you get a call, get yourself an expert on planned giving.)

Finally, when you get a bequest, set an example for others by publicizing the gift and the donor.

CHARITY SALES AND SCRIP

If you've ever bought a candy bar from a kid who came to your door on behalf of a good cause, you've participated in a charity gift sales program. We'll look briefly here at two types of these programs—charity sales and sales of scrip (whether e-scrip or so-called regular scrip).

Charity Sales

Thousands of for-profit companies make products available for nonprofits to purchase and sell. The nonprofit typically keeps 50 percent of the sale price (the percentages are lower if there is lower volume). Youth membership organizations, PTAs, and disease-related organizations are frequently successful in getting their members to sell gift wrap, cookie dough, apples, and so forth. The business logic rests on the twin premises that members feel more comfortable selling items than asking for donations and that the people approached by the organization's members are making a donation that can be justified by the purchase of a product (the donors probably wouldn't buy a candy bar from a Safeway representative stopping by). As a result, nonuseful items, such as plastic message bracelets and pins, also work for some groups. A do-it-yourself way to test the idea of charity sales is to purchase candy bars at a discount store, wrap your own printed message around them, and try to sell them.

Making money through sales requires discipline and the ability to get many people motivated to sell to their friends, their neighbors (by going door to door), and their co-workers. To make $500, you will first need to buy—and then sell—a thousand candy bars. If you have thirty members, that means thirty-four candy bars each.

Regular Scrip and E-scrip

Scrip has become a significant source of funds for many schools, sports teams, churches, and other membership organizations. A PTA, for instance, may find itself suddenly handling tens of thousands of dollars for which it may not have the systems or the degree of volunteer conscientiousness that is required. And that's where scrip comes in.

With regular scrip, a group—let's say a nonprofit preschool—buys fifty scrip booklets for $4,750 ($95 each) from a nearby grocery chain, gas station, or other business. The school sells the scrip to parents for $100 per booklet, and the parents use the scrip at the designated business. If the parents are already patrons of that business, they don't experience any difference in the level of their expenses, and the preschool nets $250 from its $4,750 investment (the typical commission for a nonprofit is 5 percent of the face value of the scrip).

E-scrip is so much easier to manage than regular scrip that its use has grown beyond schools, sports teams, and churches to community theaters, advocacy organizations, environmental groups, and other kinds of organizations. With e-scrip, a nonprofit registers with a service such as escrip.com, and the organization's members and supporters register as well, designating the nonprofit as one they wish to support. The service then uses grocery store loyalty cards (such as Safeway's) and credit card information to move 1 to 4 percent of the price of purchased items to the nonprofit as a donation. Many supporters of nonprofits see e-scrip as a painless way to donate, but others are uncomfortable either with the necessary sharing of private information (for example, telling Wal-Mart where you donate) or with the nonprofit's association with a business of which they don't approve.

One more word on scrip and e-scrip: Purchasers of scrip or users of e-scrip cannot claim a tax deduction for their scrip purchases. (And incidentally, because the donation is credited to the corporate sponsor, scrip enormously boosts the donation levels reported by grocery stores and other businesses.)

Scrip, like charity sales, often works for organizations that have committed members who are willing to ask their contacts for relatively small donations. These approaches work best for organizations that frequently see their members/sales team in person.

IN-KIND DONATIONS

An in-kind donation is a noncash donation, such as a donation of clothing, furniture, or food. In-kind donations can also include such services as dry cleaning or legal services as well as all types of volunteer time. (In this book, however, volunteer time is treated separately.)

In-kind donations are used in several ways:

- They are given to or used with human service clients (clothing for women's shelters, food for food banks and kitchens, toys for nursery schools).

- They are used in program operations (dry cleaning for a community theater, bicycles for sports programs, fixtures for a historically preserved home, supplies for an art program).

- They are used in office operations (computers, furniture, paper, cars for staff use).

- They are sold at auctions, yard sales, and plant sales or in thrift stores and other settings (cars, boats, paintings).

For some nonprofits, in-kind donations are a key strategy, both for impact and for financial sustainability. For others, the occasional donation of furniture or a fax machine supports the organization but is not a significant business line. In both cases, in-kind donations also work to increase involvement by constituents.

If in-kind donations are important for your organization, consider them a business line that must be attended to, nurtured, invested in, and monitored. For example, a homeless youth outreach organization obtains hip clothing and ready-to-eat food as donations to give to young people in the program. If this clothing and food were purchased, it would cost $60,000 per year. As a result, the program brings in $60,000 worth of donations and "spends" $60,000 on clothing and food for its clients. The executive director estimates that he spends about 5 percent of his time nurturing relationships with the business donors. From an accounting perspective, this program loses money because it brings in $60,000 and spends $64,000 ($60,000 in goods given away, and $4,000 in staff time). But the real-world perspective is that the organization nets $56,000 from this program (see Figure 10.1, which shows that the program, by virtue of its location on the Matrix Map, is a Star—a program with high impact and high profitability).

Figure 10.1
In-Kind Donations on the Matrix Map

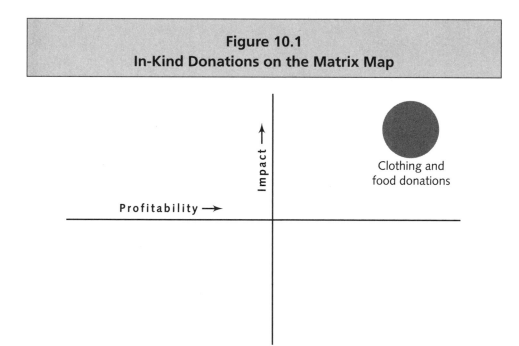

Recognizing the donation program as a Star serves to remind the organization of the program's importance, its relative size and impact within the organization, and the reasons for the organization to continue investing in it. Last year a national clothing company with a hip brand decided that its local branches could no longer donate unsold clothing directly, and this company had been a large donor to the organization. The organization realized that it needed to pay more attention to continually attracting new business donors, and it was decided that one or two new board members would be recruited to work on this task.

SUMMARY

A common reaction after seeing an organization's Matrix Map is to have the thought that the organization simply needs to raise more money. But we all know there is nothing simple about that.

As an organization explores various business lines and ways of increasing its revenue, it is helpful for board members and staff alike to have an understanding of what it takes to succeed. This chapter has explored business lines aimed at generating more traditional philanthropic support—through Internet fundraising, for example, or through major donors, direct mail, grant writing, and corporate giving.

The success of any of these business lines is increased when its requirements are matched to the strengths of an organization. For example, organizations with access to lots of names and addresses are more successful with direct mail. Organizations that have built constituent and donor loyalty over the years are more likely to succeed with a planned giving program. And organizations that are in the same city as the headquarters of a corporation and have board members and volunteers who are corporate employees are more likely to be able to increase the gifts they receive from corporations.

Raising more money is never easy. It requires an investment of time, energy, and money. But actions directed toward increasing revenue become more strategic when the needs of each business line and the strengths of the organization are understood.

Earned-Income Business Lines

This chapter on earned-income business lines, like the previous chapter on contributed-income business lines, does not attempt to cover all possible funding vehicles. Instead, we focus on a fast primer about the business logic of the earned-income vehicles that are most appropriately and most commonly used or considered by community nonprofits.

FEES FOR SERVICE: THE NONPROFIT SPECTRUM

Despite the importance of fees, not only to individual nonprofit organizations but also to the nonprofit sector as a whole, the nature of fees in the nonprofit sector is still not well understood from a strategy perspective. There is good research and literature on how to set prices, for instance, but little on seeing the spectrum of fee-generating programs as belonging to an overall strategy that maximizes both impact and financial viability.

Each of the funding models discussed in this chapter represents a particular business line's strategy for sustainability. Consider, for example, five nonprofit preschools, where the same service—early childhood education—can be sustainable at a variety of points along the spectrum of fees for service:

- Preschool A: 100 percent of tuition paid by parents
- Preschool B: 100 percent of costs paid by government (for low-income children)

151

- Preschool C: Some slots paid 100 percent by parents, some paid 100 percent by government
- Preschool D: Parent-paid tuition plus fundraising
- Preschool E: Parent-paid tuition and volunteer staffing

We might present these different funding mixes for these five preschools as shown in Figure 11.1. Each of these strategies may constitute a sustainable business model for a preschool or another kind of nonprofit organization, but the organization would require different assets and strengths to be able to handle its chosen strategy successfully.

In this chapter, we'll take a look at three major types of earned-income—consumer-paid fees, government contracts, and income from a mix of funding sources—but will actually discuss five funding models, given that the organization using a mix of funding sources may obtain revenue from direct payers in combination with government contracts, from direct payers in combination with fundraising, and from direct payers in combination with the efforts of volunteers.

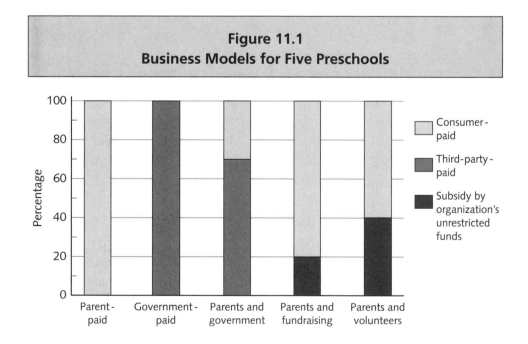

Figure 11.1
Business Models for Five Preschools

Consumer-Paid Fees

Similar to the traditional for-profit model, the consumer-paid fee-for-service model is a very attractive one for a nonprofit—if it is serving a community that can afford to pay for the services. This model is also common among organizations that may run business or social enterprises that don't necessarily have a direct relationship to organizational mission.

The organization that succeeds with this type of strategy typically has a very good understanding of the market it serves—the needs of its potential customers as well as the nature of its competitors in the area. For-profit companies with multiple outlets may be able to provide the service more cheaply because of their greater number of locations, and they may undercut the price that the nonprofit charges. To protect against this situation, nonprofits need to focus on costs while ensuring a high quality of service.

A programmatic risk for consumer-paid services is that this strategy can shift programs toward serving a higher-income population that may not be the program's intended group of beneficiaries. The Matrix Map helps us understand the interplay of impact and profitability in a sliding scale program. For instance, imagine a mental health counseling agency with a sliding scale based on ability to pay. Low-income clients pay $10 per visit, whereas people at the top of the sliding scale pay $75 per visit. Let's say that the costs for the organization are $75 per visit. If the organization has clients spread out across the sliding scale, it may find that it needs $25,000 per year to subsidize the below-cost clients. But if most clients are paying at the low end of the sliding scale, the organization needs more in subsidies. This situation may arise if others (including for-profit therapists) start offering higher-end services at higher prices, thus taking away clients at the high end of the sliding scale. Conversely, if the organization focuses on clients who can pay at the top of the sliding scale, the program may have less impact if the organization's mission is focused on serving lower-income populations (see Figure 11.2).

Government Contracts

By some estimates, government contracts represent approximately 40 percent of the nonprofit sector's total income. The scale of government funding means that this kind of funding is typically the vehicle for increasing the volume of services (sometimes referred to as *going to scale*).

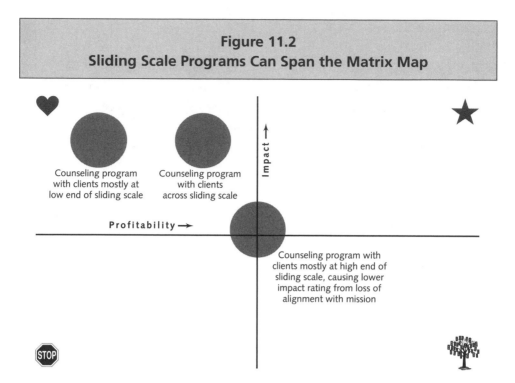

Figure 11.2
Sliding Scale Programs Can Span the Matrix Map

Counseling program with clients mostly at low end of sliding scale

Counseling program with clients across sliding scale

Impact →

Profitability →

Counseling program with clients mostly at high end of sliding scale, causing lower impact rating from loss of alignment with mission

Government contracts come from all levels of government—federal, state, county, city, and other levels. Government funding usually comes in the form of what is called *categorical funding*, that is, funding streams identified by topic (such as education, domestic violence, neighborhood revitalization, disabilities, veterinary research, and so forth). Three typical types of contract structures have the following characteristics:

• *Cost reimbursement*, whereby the organization performs a service and then invoices and is reimbursed for its costs (these costs are negotiated in advance, often at the line-item level)

• *Fee for service*, whereby services are offered at an agreed-upon rate (such as a rate for each person who stays at a homeless shelter for a night, or for each person for whom a job has been obtained)

• *Grants*, whereby funds are awarded for a sizable project as a whole, often in the areas of research or large-scale program development

Government contracts are typically large (by comparison with foundation and corporate grants), renewable, and directed to the core services of an organization. For example, if an organization provides education for four hundred children with disabilities, its main source of funding is likely to be government because other sources are unlikely to be able to award funding at that level.

It takes time—sometimes years—to obtain government funding. Sometimes a proposal for funding can be approved but not funded, which means that the government agency likes the idea and the proposal but is not going to appropriate the funds to make it possible.

Proposals for government funding can get caught up in political disputes, in crossfire between competing city departments, or in attacks on politicians who support the proposals. An organization may also be asked to help a government agency on a related project, a request that some may interpret as reflecting an extension of the organization's mission while others see it as an unethical request for a favor. The public nature of government contracts means that an organization's failure to perform on a contract is far more likely to get into the newspaper than would be failure to perform on a foundation grant. The organization that is successful over time with government funding excels not only in program delivery and documentation but also in alertness to the political environment and ability to stay on good terms with politicians across the political spectrum (see Table 11.1).

Mix of Revenue from Direct Payers and Other Sources

A strategy that many nonprofits employ is to mix earned income with other revenue strategies for purposes of either mission or money. In these cases, greater access to services may be achieved if, for example, government subsidies for

TABLE 11.1 Funding Through Government Contracts	
Key Advantage	Large and renewable, often for core services
Requirements	Sufficient cash reserves to cover lags in payment
	Strong ability to monitor and document costs and activities
	Political awareness and involvement
Risks	Limits on overhead, which may mean that the contract does not cover the entire cost of delivery
	Possible restrictions that contradict the organization's values or mission

low-income users are combined with client fees from those who can pay. This section describes three examples of such mixed-payer strategies: use of direct payers and government, use of direct payers and fundraising, and use of direct payers and volunteers.

Direct Payers and Government Contracts   This revenue strategy combines revenues from those who can pay directly for services with third-party revenues from government on behalf of those who can't afford to pay for services. The advantage of this model is that the organization has an additional revenue source to cover costs that may not be covered by a government contract. Many organizations can be successful with this type of strategy, but it carries its own unique risks for program quality with respect to retaining constituents who are paying for themselves (see Table 11.2). Oftentimes when competition opens up in the community, competitors try to attract people who are paying for themselves, and the organization that uses a mix of direct payers and government is forced to adjust its model. One way to protect against this situation is to understand the market and constituents' needs and ensure that the programs offered are of top quality.

Direct Payers and Fundraising   Subsidizing direct payers with fundraising is a traditional model that many childcare facilities and private schools employ. It works best when constituents are engaged in the organization, have means or connections to those with means, and have a stake in the health of the organization. The organization can also use this strategy successfully even if the payers cannot

TABLE 11.2 Funding Through a Mix of Direct Payers and Government Contracts	
Key Advantage	Ability to subsidize government funding
Requirements	Political awareness about government contracts
	Cash reserves
	Understanding of the market, including competitive position and constituents' needs
Risk	Competition for constituents who pay for themselves

directly contribute more. In these cases, it is helpful if the organization plays a vital role in the community and has a board that is engaged in the community and can reach out and tap into the philanthropic market. Fundraising strategies can include individuals or foundations, depending on the strengths of the organization. The typical risks associated with philanthropic fundraising include mission drift, downturns in the economy, and uneven cash flows (see Table 11.3).

Direct Payers and Volunteer Efforts Combining revenue from direct payers with the efforts of volunteers is a model used by many social enterprises, such as the traditional coffee shop that also provides job training, or the consignment shop that resells clothes and other items and is staffed by volunteers. This revenue strategy works best when the organization has a large corps of volunteers to draw from, and when either the skills required of those volunteers are minimal or training is provided. One risk is hidden costs that, once a volunteer program is implemented, are not so hidden. These include costs for volunteer recruitment, training, coordination, and recognition. Finding the right volunteers and retaining them can be time consuming and expensive, but it can also result in payroll savings (see Table 11.4).

Table 11.3 Funding Through a Mix of Direct Payers and Fundraising	
Key Advantage	Ability for fundraising to subsidize contributions of direct payers
Requirement	Connection to philanthropic market, through either the board or constituents of the organization
Risks	Mission drift (fundraising side is allowed to drive the organization) Cash flow challenges

Table 11.4 Funding Through a Mix of Direct Payers and Volunteer Efforts	
Key Advantage	Cost effectiveness of using volunteers
Requirements	Pool of volunteers with appropriate skills to draw from Program for volunteer recruitment, training, and retention
Risk	Potential unreliability of volunteers

SUMMARY

Earned-revenue strategies can be very enticing for nonprofits that are looking for an antidote to asking for money, which traditional fundraising requires. But the fee-for-service model also has its challenges. Nonprofits must understand the needs of whoever is providing the funding and must keep a sharp eye on the market. In many cases, for-profits or other organizations with lower costs come into an area and diminish a nonprofit's client load. In other cases, a nonprofit's core constituents may not have the money to pay for services. In these cases, it is very common to subsidize revenue from direct payers with government contracts, fundraising, or the efforts of volunteers. Each strategy requires different strengths, and most nonprofits use a hybrid approach, relying on contributed philanthropic support and earned income so they can be sustainable at any given time. As an organization analyzes its Matrix Map, it should consider its strengths and seek revenue strategies that build on them.

PART FIVE

Ongoing Decision Making and Leadership

At the beginning of this book, we defined sustainability as an orientation rather than a destination. But staying oriented to the same direction doesn't mean traveling in a straight line. A person going north will need to zigzag along the way, to find the pass through the mountains or cross rivers—or, in more modern terms, to take a faster interstate. In short, having a compass that points north isn't enough. Staying on course requires constant observation, constant mapping, and constant decision making.

In a similar way, today's leaders are tested by their ability to make decisions in a rapidly changing landscape, and with constantly changing capacity. Making ongoing decisions to refine or, if necessary, dramatically change a nonprofit business model is the hard work of senior staff and boards. As we think about the kinds of significant decisions that the Matrix Map calls for—from transferring a beloved but dated program to choosing a new program director to increasing the impact of a moneymaker—it is worth considering the specific nature of decision making, with a particular awareness of the realities of community nonprofit culture.

In Chapter Twelve, we explore how the Matrix Map can be integrated into a strategic planning process. Chapter Thirteen examines decision making and the role of leadership.

The Matrix Map and Strategic Planning

S trategic planning often has both planning and choice-making aspects. The planning process offers a chance to pause and think, to try out new ideas and scenarios, to debate, and perhaps to reach consensus among a new group of board and staff members working in a new phase of the organization's trajectory. Strategic plans often express choices about what the organization will focus on and what it won't take up. Because the Matrix Map is a tool for choice making, it naturally fits well into a strategic planning process. In the context of such a process, the Matrix Map can be particularly useful in certain situations, and in a variety of ways:

• *To illustrate to board and staff members what the organization is already doing as the first stage in planning.* Despite staff meetings and program reports at board meetings, staff and board members often have a weak grasp of the organization's activities as a whole. Starting with a quickly drawn Matrix Map helps everyone understand what the organization really does and what its current business model is—a crucial platform for strategic planning.

• *To inform and focus data gathering.* Strategic planning processes often obtain external data as an environmental scan early in the process, creating a broad backdrop for the planning discussions. For instance, donors might be surveyed to see what they value most about a nonprofit. If, prior to data gathering, the Matrix Map is used to identify areas as possible priorities, the survey can be more focused. And if, using the Matrix Map, the organization identifies planned giving as a possible Money Tree for the organization, the survey can focus on testing approaches to planned giving with donors. If the Matrix Map identifies a program as a Stop Sign, the external data work can zero in on possible partners to whom the program can be transferred.

• *To prioritize among many worthy goals.* Strategic plans typically focus on establishing goals, but it's harder for a plan to distinguish between areas where the organization can be more effective than in other areas—often because of funding opportunities. Rather than pit money against goals in a no-win contest, the Matrix Map helps an organization illustrate how it is pursuing multiple goals in a way that is informed by financial choices, but not dominated by them. Priorities are not based solely on mission worthiness but on the understanding of an activity's role in the organization's overall strategy for sustainability.

• *To ensure that financial concerns are integrated into the strategic plan.* Surprising as it may be, many strategic plans hardly mention money or sustainability. At the end of an arduous process, the organization has a new mission statement and an ambitious plan for impact but no real plan for how to get the money that will make that plan a reality. In other cases, the plan for funding is based more on wishful thinking than on ideas tested for their viability. In such instances, a Matrix Map that illustrates the new strategic plan will typically show many Hearts and Money Trees, thus drawing attention to examining whether the projections for Money Trees are realistic.

• *As a reality check.* Sometimes an organization gets lost in the details of many documents and finds itself being drawn by details into an area where no one expected or intended to go. Given the work that has already gone into the planning process, people are naturally reluctant to rethink the big pieces. Illustrating the draft strategic plan as a Matrix Map is an easy way to see whether the organization pictured is really an organization that board and staff members want and can believe in.

BUILDING A STRATEGIC PLANNING PROCESS WITH THE MATRIX MAP

A much appreciated strength of strategic planning processes is that they clarify an organization's vision and goals and develop consensus about a general direction.

A common weakness of strategic plans is that they either neglect financial strategies or, at the other extreme, overemphasize financial choices.

One way to bring financial sustainability front and center in a strategic planning process—without simply following the money—is to use the Matrix Map as a tool for the process. Bringing the Matrix Map to a strategic planning process need not change the traditional process entirely. Two simple changes bring in the core ideas of relative impact, relative financial implications, and decision making that intertwines impact and concerns about financial sustainability.

The first change is to broaden the discussion of fundraising goals and plans to a discussion of plans and goals for revenue generation. In many nonprofits, programs that rely on designated funds—such as government-funded or corporate-funded programs—are kept in the plan but are not scrutinized for their impact. In addition, because the strategic plan is often initiated as a way to engage the board (usually in fundraising), strategic plans tend to focus on board-driven fundraising ideas rather than on the organization's total revenue picture. For instance, a nonprofit journal may develop a strategic plan that includes more individual donations solicited by board members, but it neglects the role of subscription revenue—and the role of board members in obtaining subscribers.

The second change is related to external data gathering. In a typical strategic plan, external data gathering—in the form of interviews with stakeholders, for example, or a scan of competitors—is conducted to develop a general background picture of the environment in which the organization works. By changing the data scan from one of broad-picture development to one of testing assumptions and opportunities around both impact and finance, the organization can make more focused use of the time it has for gathering information. Exhibit 12.1 shows what a typical strategic planning process using the Matrix Map may look like.

Exhibit 12.1. A Strategic Planning Process That Uses the Matrix Map

- *Step 1. Creating the organization's current Matrix Map.* This step illustrates the organization's current business model in addition to showing the relative impacts of programs and their relative profitability.

(Continued)

- *Step 2. Establishing the organization's vision, mission, and goals.* Use one of the many processes identified with strategic planning.

- *Step 3. Analyzing relative impact and relative profitability.* What changes are desired in the current business model? On the basis of the newly stated vision, mission, and goals, the organization revisits the relative impact ratings and draws the Matrix Map again, this time with the new criteria. Individually and as a group, leaders confront the strategic imperatives and write a business model statement.

- *Step 4. Gathering of data on the external environment to test perceptions of impact and markets.* Identify the questions that arose in the examination of strategic imperatives, and shape data gathering to respond to those questions. For example, determine whether the organization is in fact the only provider of services to a certain population group, or seek a partner to whom a program can be divested, or look at the competitive market for a service and for what current prices are.

- *Step 5. Revising the Matrix Map as the strategic plan.* With the data in hand, and having had time to sleep on all this information, organizational leaders can now revisit the strategic imperatives with new information. The desired Matrix Map can be drawn to reflect decisions about activities, and the new picture can be reviewed for overall organizational impact and financial sustainability.

- *Step 6. Writing up the narrative of the strategic plan.* With the newly stated vision and mission, a business model statement, the decisions that have been made about various activities, and a Matrix Map that captures those decisions, a narrative can easily be written up to conform to whatever format has been chosen as the most useful one.

In short, through this process the Matrix Map becomes a central tool for the decision making that needs to occur in strategic planning. It becomes the platform for discussions of impact as well as for financial viability. Like all good tools, it doesn't make decisions for the organization. Rather, it illuminates the implications of various choices so that the organization can take them into account in other parts of the plan.

CIRCUMSTANCES ESPECIALLY SUITED TO USE OF THE MATRIX MAP

The Matrix Map is designed to be useful both as an everyday mental reference and as a tool in a structured group setting. But there are some particular circumstances that suggest the use of the Matrix Map:

• *When there's a new executive.* For a new executive director, developing a Matrix Map provides a fast way to understand how the organization's pieces fit together. As a new executive comes on board, board and staff members are often eager—or at least ready—to consider changes to the business model and to programming. The process of considering relative impacts and profitability gives the organization a chance to reflect on its current business model and priorities and, together with the new executive, to look at possible changes.

• *When there's increased urgency regarding the strategic plan.* Sometimes a strategic planning process has come up with some bold new ideas, but it's not clear to everyone how the organization will go about implementing them. For instance, a strategic plan may include such goals as increasing earned income or reducing the size of the budget strategically rather than through across-the-board cuts. Staff members may have a hard time knowing how to get started on such projects. The Matrix Map will often point to where action will be most effective.

• *When the management team needs a leadership development process.* Management teams typically discuss the coordination of operations, but they seldom discuss which programs are more effective than others, or even which attributes of a program the organization considers most and least valuable. In reality, individual members of the management team may have ideas about the relative worth of various programs and activities, but they don't have a way to raise these issues. As a result, priorities are often discussed in the surrogate discussion about the budget. Bringing the conversation to the management team is partly a group learning experience where assumptions are raised, debated, and considered. Full consensus may not be reached, but the elements of impact will have entered the team's purview. In addition, when management team members understand the role that a program plays in an organization, they can guide it in the right direction. For example, rather than assuming that all programs are supposed to grow, they can see why one program is being kept fairly small (because it's a Heart and its costs are being contained), or why another program needs attention to strengthening its quality and impact.

• *When there's a need for planning at the departmental or program level.* The Matrix Map works well for particular program areas as well as for the organization as a whole. For example, consider a music department in a large nonprofit educational organization. The department may offer music classes to those who want to learn how to play instruments and to those who want to learn how to write music. The classes may be aimed at different age groups or centered on different instruments or different styles of music. Even with all these offerings, the music department as a whole typically has a financial goal that it has to achieve while having a high impact. Once again, the Matrix Map shows how all these individual pieces work together to help the department reach that goal. In addition, by monitoring the Matrix Map over time, the organization's leaders may see that interest in certain classes has dropped over time as reflected in those classes' declining profitability, since classes are funded through a fee-for-service strategy. The declining revenue may be a signal that the department should offer some new and different classes. At the same time, the new classes may take a little while to catch on with the organization's constituents, and the Matrix Map helps give leaders the discipline they need in order to see how many new Heart classes the organization can afford.

THE MATRIX MAP AND BUSINESS PLANNING

When nonprofit people hear the term *business planning for nonprofits*, they often think of it as defining a plan for earned income. In other instances, a business plan is understood to be something developed for new projects—a feasibility plan that projects activities, costs, and revenues. In still other cases, a nonprofit may see its business plan as simply its budget for the next year or two.

In the for-profit world, business plans are typically drafted and completed as part of the process of obtaining capital, whether start-up investments or loans to grow or sustain operations. In other words, the purpose of the business plan is to obtain funding, and it is often organized as a public relations–oriented document rather than as a plan that will be followed to the letter. As a result, business plans are often legitimately derided as wildly optimistic works of fiction.

If nonprofit strategic plans tend to neglect financial sustainability, nonprofit business plans tend to neglect programmatic impact. Business planning consultants often simplistically urge nonprofits simply to do what's profitable and drop what's not.

Business planning also suffers from some of the same problems as strategic planning. Plans have to be based on assumptions, and as assumptions change, the plans can quickly become irrelevant or obsolete. And all too often the assumptions tend to be conventional assumptions that can overlook the most important factors. A typical example might involve a scientific organization whose lead biologist also has an interest in botany and has been able to get funding for some interesting botany research, but a key assumption that has gone unexamined is this biologist's continued tenure. In this example, the scientist's interest in botany is an individual rather than an institutional asset. Or, to take another example, a school uses its gym after hours to offer a fitness program for adults. The program has been successful for many years, but the city has just opened up a community center three blocks away where fitness classes are offered at a lower price. The school program's customer base dries up overnight, even though the school's need for this additional revenue continues. The business plan for the school's fitness program did consider the more expensive fitness alternatives available in the area but did not identify one of its key assumptions—that there would never be another community-centered, affordable facility to compete with it for customers.

Business plans excel when they insightfully explain the market as well as the interplay between operations (how the program actually gets carried out) and the requirements for success. In particular, business plans often appropriately point to specific individuals and to how important they are to obtaining funding, to operational success, and to marketing. In contrast, nonprofits tend to underemphasize the importance of specific individuals in crucial leadership positions.

The Matrix Map is a good supplement to exercises in business planning. It sets the stage for business planning by illustrating the de facto business model that is already in place. The Matrix Map doesn't diminish financial concerns, but it does bring in programmatic concerns in an understandable way. By focusing on the business *model*, the Matrix Map readily supports the projections in the business *plan*.

SUMMARY

Strategic plans, like all other plans, are based on working assumptions about what the future will be like. The organization, thinking of the future as a kind of canvas, chooses what to paint on it. The Matrix Map is an ideal tool to integrate into the planning process. Not only does it help integrate the revenue strategies necessary for sustainability into the strategic discussion, it also lays out a framework for making decisions. Furthermore, by using the Matrix Map as part of planning, an organization can also use it in ongoing decision making as it responds to the changing environment during implementation of the plan.

Decision Making and Leadership

Over the past ten years, the nonprofit sector has increased its attention to nonprofit leadership exponentially. We have seen the emergence of myriad leadership programs and frameworks meant to identify, develop, and sustain current and next-generation leaders. These efforts are critical; they have helped raise the profile and capacity of our sector's leadership. And yet, just as strategic and business planning theory has tended to neglect the interdependence of impact and profit, too many nonprofit leadership frameworks neglect the fundamental responsibility of a nonprofit executive to pursue and maintain sustainability. Not only is there a skill set required to this—strong skills in financial analysis, for instance—but taking that responsibility seriously is also a fundamental orientation of nonprofit leadership. And since sustainability is never permanent, this ongoing pursuit in practice comes down to effective decision making.

The Matrix Map featured in this book is a tool to facilitate the necessary decision making. To further support leaders' shift to a decision-making orientation, this closing chapter reflects on the importance of successful execution and on the nature of the difficult decisions that leaders with an orientation of sustainability have to make all the time.

chapter THIRTEEN

DEFINING EXECUTION

We see successful execution as, first, getting things done. It's easy to recognize the person who has exciting plans but can never seem to get anything accomplished. Perhaps less visible is the person who gets a lot done, but without a written document titled "Plan." Getting things done—execution—is a skill, an attitude, and a strategic advantage. For-profit business plans have good reasons for designating specific individuals who will be in charge of getting things done. Even a great plan will be at risk without key individuals who are driven to deliver.

And yet getting things done is not enough, of course. Successful execution also means getting work done with high quality and technical excellence. Organizations that lean toward being good enough rather than striving for technical excellence are often the ones that fade over time, unable to sustain funding relationships or staff and board members who expect higher standards. We use the term *technical excellence* here rather than *excellence* to emphasize the rigor and discipline that must complement passion and caring so as to create exemplary work. Technically excellent work is research work that is rigorous, not slapdash. It is hospice work that combines caring volunteers with strong training and medical support. It is embodied in a nonprofit art gallery that not only supports local artists but also demands artistic excellence from them.

Rigorous execution is also how we learn whether our plans were the right ones, and how they should be continuously adapted—or even abandoned. In other words, we learn by doing and refining between episodic planning processes. We believe that the well-developed practices around planning in our sector must now be accompanied by a framework for execution and decision making. The overall strategic direction developed during episodic planning is a critical guidepost, but what leaders do every day is make decisions that, over time, amount to the *actual* rather than the *planned* financial health and mission impact of their organizations.

Figure 13.1 illustrates this evolution in thinking. The old paradigm is to plan and then implement the plan, and then plan again. The new paradigm is to use intensive episodic planning, as called for, and then to focus on strong execution, learning, and decision making to maintain impact and financial health in real time.

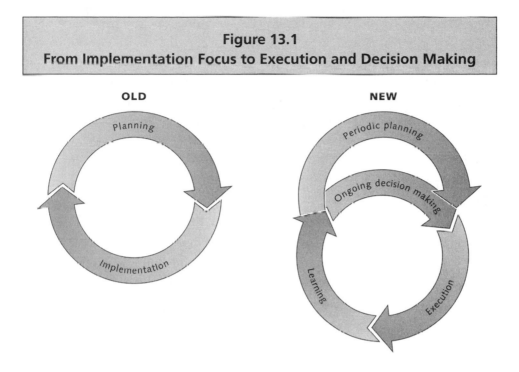

Figure 13.1
From Implementation Focus to Execution and Decision Making

OLD

Planning

Implementation

NEW

Periodic planning

Ongoing decision making

Learning

Execution

THE CHALLENGES OF DECISION MAKING

One reason why planning is such a comfortable exercise is that it often focuses on setting goals rather than making hard choices. But when senior staff and board members decide to make a meaningful change to their organizational business model in the pursuit of sustainability—perhaps a Matrix Map inspired choice—they are not just deciding to change the business model. They are deciding to change the organization. Deciding to spin off a Stop Sign to another organization may entail laying off staff and using the money saved to hire new, differently skilled staff. Deciding to invest in a Star may mean being ruthless about quality—perhaps letting go of some so-so staff to hire higher performers. Investing in a Star may mean recruiting board members who are different from those currently in place. These kinds of decisions have two important requirements.

First, strategic decision making requires judgment. More than ever, today's decisions involve trade-offs and risks. Data and disciplined decision-making processes can help us do a better job of identifying those trade-offs and risks upfront, but judgment will always be an essential component. In particular, the development of impact and financial criteria is a strong way to support judgment. But in any given situation, or with any Matrix Map, the choice of options will seldom be straightforward or completely data-based. Acknowledging the key role of judgment is part of an orientation toward effective decision making.

Second, strategic decision making requires leadership. Decisions seldom emerge on their own. Leaders must drive the pace of decision making, and they must lead—and sometimes drag—the organization through strategic crossroads. Leaders don't just facilitate consensus-building discussions. Leaders must frame the problem, signal viable solutions, get feedback, revise, and resignal, in an iterative process.

Have you ever heard it said of someone that he or she just can't make the hard decisions? What makes a decision tough or hard? A hard decision isn't hard the same way a math problem is hard. We can be better at making tough decisions if we understand the components of what makes them hard:

• *Hardship.* Tough decisions usually result in difficulties for people—perhaps patients who can't come in on Saturdays anymore, or the layoff of a staff person. Managers are understandably reluctant to commit to such decisions.

• *Trade-offs.* Most decisions involve both positive and negative outcomes. We make them because we believe that the positives outweigh the negatives. A decision to cut staff benefits will result in lower staff morale as well as cost savings. A decision to cancel theater performances will result in loss of community presence and delivery of less program impact. As a result of some decisions, certain staff will thrive with new opportunities while others will lose influence and stature.

• *Risk.* Some decisions are hard to make because they involve risk. Deciding to hold a first-ever fundraising event is a decision to take a risk. The event can result in needed funds, but at the risk of a net loss. Borrowing money may be the right decision to meet payroll while waiting for a promised grant, but if the grant is cancelled or delayed, it may mean that we have allowed spending that later can't be recouped.

• *Lack of complete information.* If we had all the information we need about the future, decision making would be easy! Had many arts groups seen the recession coming, they would not have embarked on what are now stalled capital projects.

A deeper reality is that many of these tough decisions would be easy for leaders to make if everyone in the organization were in complete agreement about them.

For instance, such decisions as when to lay off staff or close a program or merge with another organization would be relatively easy to make if everyone were on the same page. But consensus is rarely the reality with decisions as complex and risky as these.

Hard decisions don't have consensus at their backs. Hard decisions are often unpopular. We in the nonprofit sector often rely on consensus—or at least the perception of it—to test whether we are making the right decision. Indeed, many leaders are unaccustomed to acting decisively in the absence of consensus. But as decisions need to be made faster, there is less time for consensus to develop. Further, the complexity of some decisions probably renders consensus impossible, given the variety of perspectives that people hold across a board and a staff. As a result, leaders are making more decisions in situations where consensus hasn't formed and may never form.

SUMMARY

Leadership is about effective decision making, and the Matrix Map is a powerful tool to support leaders in making sustainability-related decisions. Recognizing that decision making is not the same as planning is important. Indeed, leaders need to focus their time and attention on the execution and decision making that come between episodic planning if they want to ensure a healthy, high-impact nonprofit organization. In the end, no matter the quality of the data or the seeming clarity of the business model imperatives, continuous decision making requires judgment about inevitable trade-offs, and it requires strong leadership.

Getting to Nonprofit Sustainability

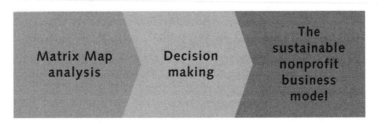

Matrix Map analysis → Decision making → The sustainable nonprofit business model

CONCLUDING WORDS

The leaders of today's community-based organizations are expected to run successful hybrid businesses—to be facile at acquiring and maintaining an array of earned and contributed funding streams. Moreover, they are expected to produce measurable results for their constituents and funders. These interrelated challenges require a move away from a charity business model as well as from the planning assumptions and processes that have historically been sufficient to support that model.

Today's effective leaders hold impact and financial return in an integrated way, all the time. They are also clear on the distinct needs and frameworks for planning, decision making, and execution—never overvaluing planning to the neglect of execution, learning, and continuous decision making. The sustainability orientation and the Matrix Map tool that we offer in this book are meant to support these complex and demanding leadership responsibilities.

We know from our work with leaders all over the country that the struggle for sustainability—for deep impact and adequate working capital—has never been more challenging, and that the societal need for the work of nonprofits has never been greater. We commend the leaders who take this challenge on and, in so doing, engage people in solving problems and strengthening communities. Our hope is that this book will aid them in their ongoing pursuit of sustainable organizations and impact.

BOOKS

Balanced Scorecard: Step-by-Step for Government and Nonprofit Agencies (Wiley, 2008)
Written by Paul Niven, this book is a guide to adopting the Balanced Scorecard tool in nonprofit and public sector agencies. The Balanced Scorecard is a tool for forming strategy and measuring results. It considers financial return along with mission alignment and other interdependent strategy elements.

Competitive Strategy: Techniques for Analyzing Industries and Competitors (Free Press, 1980)
Written by Michael Porter, this classic management text provides a framework for developing competitive strategy. It instructs the reader in how to analyze an industry overall and specific competitors therein.

Financial Leadership for Nonprofit Executives: Guiding Your Organization to Long-Term Success (Fieldstone Alliance, 2005)
Written by Jeanne Bell and Elizabeth Schaffer, this book is for senior staff and executives at community nonprofits and focuses on the principles of financial leadership. It provides a comprehensive case study outlining financial statement analysis, annual budgeting, and quality reporting to staff and board.

Financing Nonprofits: Putting Theory into Practice (AltaMira Press, 2008)
Edited by Dennis Young, this book includes chapters by sector experts on the various forms of financing available to nonprofits, including donations, in-kind contributions, debt, and so on. The editor also offers guiding principles on combining revenue streams to achieve financial viability.

Judgment in Managerial Decision Making (Wiley, 1997)
Written by Max Bazerman, this academic book will be appreciated by nonprofit practitioners as an overview of different schools of thought and of various frameworks about group decision making in organizations.

The Nonprofit Strategy Revolution (Fieldstone Alliance, 2008)

Written by David La Piana, this guide includes a cogent critique of traditional strategic planning and walks readers through what the author calls "real-time strategic planning." The book includes extensive references to business models, financial analysis, and sustainability.

Perspectives on Strategy from the Boston Consulting Group (Wiley, 1998)

Edited by Carl Stern and George Stalk Jr., this is a compendium of seventy-five short articles by members of BCG, the renowned business strategy consulting firm. Themes include the development, practice, and measurement of business strategy.

Strategic Planning for Nonprofit Organizations (Wiley, 2005)

Written by Mike Allison and Jude Kaye, and now in its second edition, this practical guide and workbook walks readers step by step through the strategic planning process. The book includes references to the use of dual-bottom-line thinking as part of planning for financial viability.

PRINT AND ONLINE PERIODICALS

Blue Avocado

This influential online publication with sixty thousand subscribers is edited by Jan Masaoka and contains practical and provocative articles on finance, strategy, human resource management, governance, and other issues of immediate relevance to nonprofit staff and volunteers (www.blueavocado.org).

Harvard Business Review

Published by the Harvard Business School, this is the preeminent business management and leadership periodical and frequently publishes articles relevant to nonprofits (http://hbr.org).

The Nonprofit Quarterly

This quarterly periodical is published specifically for the leaders of community-based nonprofits. Its editorial goal is to provide a forum for the critical thinking and exploration needed to help nonprofits stay true to their democratic calling—and to achieve their potential as effective, powerful, and influential organizations in concert with their constituencies. It frequently publishes articles on nonprofit strategy and finance (www.nonprofitquarterly.org).

The Stanford Social Innovation Review

This quarterly publication out of Stanford University focuses on social innovation ideas from businesses, foundations, and nonprofits (www.ssireview.org).

WEB RESOURCES

The Bridgespan Group

This consulting firm's Web site features useful articles and case studies focused on nonprofit business planning and innovation (www.bridgespan.org).

Nonprofit Finance Fund

The Web site of this national nonprofit lender and financial consulting and training organization has useful articles and case studies on business models, financing, capital projects, and business planning (www.nonprofitfinancefund.org).

Spectrum Nonprofit Services

Spectrum Nonprofit Services offers online and in-person trainings and consulting services in strategy, finance, and the Matrix Map (www.spectrumnonprofit.com).

ACKNOWLEDGMENTS

A central piece of this book—the Matrix Map—is an adaptation of the Growth-Share Matrix, originally developed by the Boston Consulting Group and sometimes known as the BCG matrix. In that matrix, the axes are market share and growth rates; despite our using different axes, our debt to the BCG matrix is obvious and immeasurable. Over time, there have been several adaptations of the BCG matrix, and these have brought in different or additional variables. One of these adaptations is the McMillan Matrix, developed by Ian McMillan for government and nonprofit organizations, which uses four criteria: alignment with mission statement, competitive position, program attractiveness, and alternative coverage.

Other matrix tools that we have found useful include the TOWS (Threats Opportunities Weaknesses Strengths) Matrix developed by Heinz Weihrich; a three-dimensional model using Mission, Money, and Merit, by Kersti Krug and Charles Weinberg; and balanced scorecard approaches from a variety of authors. Our work has been informed by all these models, and we owe them a debt of gratitude as well.

We also want to thank the many nonprofit organizations that have chosen us individually and together as their consultants in the areas of financial strategies, planning, organization design, fundraising, and boards of directors. We have been honored to work with many wise and thoughtful executive directors, management team members, board members, and fellow consultants as they and we have evolved planning practices and decision-making structures. Together with many of our clients, we have put the Matrix Map into practice and refined it, and the development of this tool has been greatly helped by our clients' patience, insight, and feedback.

In particular, we also want to thank CompassPoint Nonprofit Services, its board of directors, and its funders. CompassPoint has been the university where we have all been privileged to learn and grow, in ways that are possible only with far-seeing practitioners on the board, with unrestricted funding that permits reflection and experimentation, and with colleagues who are not only committed to technical excellence but also generous in spirit.

August 2010

Jeanne Bell
San Francisco, California

Jan Masaoka
San Francisco, California

Steve Zimmerman
Milwaukee, Wisconsin

INDEX

A

ACLU, 145

Activities. *See* Business lines (core activities)

Administration costs: allocation to business line, 33–34; closing a program impact on, 84–85; description of, 31; Matrix Map for making decisions related to, 119–121

Amazon advertising, 130–131

Annual appeals: business logic of, 135; description of, 135; logistics of successful, 137–138; who to ask and timing of, 136

Annual campaign (Midtown Multiservice Center), 104

Annual street festival (Midtown Multiservice Center), 104, 118

B

Board members: direct mail role of, 139; major gifts and role of, 134; Matrix Map used to illustrate planning to, 161; things to consider for the, 8–9; weighting impact role by, 53. *See also* Executive director/CEO; Leadership

Business lines (core activities): description of, 20; determining full costs of, 30–34; determining revenue to, 31, 34–36; earned-income, 151–158; Everest Environmentalists assignment of revenue by, 37; identifying the, 20–22; leverage of, 45–46; Matrix Map with cluster of, 69

Business lines costs: analyzing merger impact on, 125; considerations for the finance staff, 33–34; direct costs, 30–31, 33–34; Everest Environmentalists full, 32; fair share of administrative costs, 31, 33–34, 84–85, 119–121; fair share of common or shared costs, 31, 33–34, 84–85

Business model: business model statement, 62–68; for five preschools, 151–152; mission and mission statements, 24–25, 41–42, 63–65. *See also* Nonprofit business model

Business model statement: definition of, 62; using Matrix Maps with, 62–65, 67–68; Midtown Multiservice Center, 63–65; samples of, 65–66; Tempest Theater, 62–63

PROGRAM SUSTAINABILITY

A. SHORE UP PROGRAM SUPPORT WITHIN YOUR ORG.

  * QUID PRO QUO — IF YOU HAVE HAD SUCCESS,
    INFORM ORG LEADERS SO INFO CAN BE USED
    FOR ORG SUS.

  * DAMAGE CONTROL/PRE EMPTIVE WARNING — IF YOU
    (OR ARE PERCEIVED AS UNSUCCESSFUL)
    HAVE NOT HAD SUCCESS AND IT IS HURTING YOU
    IN THE ORG, YOU NEED TO KNOW SO YOU CAN
    CORRECT THE PROBLEM OR MIS PERCEPTION OR
    MOVE TO ANOTHER STRATEGY.

B. ~~FOCUS ON FUNDING~~ KNOW THE FULL COST OF
   YOUR PROGRAM FOR YOUR ORG

C. ~~FOCUS ON FUND~~ DETERMINE THE CORE &
   ESSENTIAL ELEMENTS OF PROGRAM TO CONTINUE OR
   SUSTAIN.

D. FOCUS ON FUNDRAISING ACTIVITIES YOU CAN DO.
     GRANT RESEARCH & WRITING
     SPECIAL EVENTS

E. ~~EXAMINE~~ EXPLORE PARTNERS WHO CAN TAKE ON
   CORE ELEMENTS & BUILD REAL TRANSITIONS TO
   FACILITATE TRANSFER.